Sonatine Secrets

A Creative Approach to Developing Technique and Musicality

By Joy J. Song

SPi is the world's first trademark of a patented teaching method that teaches music through icons.

Contact Us
pianojoysong@gmail.com

SNS
youtube.com/c/JoySongTV
instagram.com/drsongpianoiconpedagogy
facebook.com/Dr.JoySong

Icons Design + Method **Patented**
Included: 588 Icon Stickers

Free Sample Lectures

Korea Institute of Piano Pedagogy

KIPP's mission is to spread good music through effortless teaching and fun learning, based on the words
"You will know the truth, and the truth will set you free."
(John 8:32)

KIPP's website contains a variety of useful information, such as Dr. Song's video lectures, seminars and lessons, publications and a directory of studios and teachers who teach Dr. Song's method.

Sonatine Secrets
A Creative Approach to Developing Technique and Musicality

Published by	KIPP(Korea Institute of Piano Pedagogy), Distributed by Hal Leonard
Address	7777 west Bluemound Road, Milwaukee, Wisconsin 53213
Phone	414-774-3630
Fax	414-774-3259
Web site	www.halleonard.com

Publisher	Joy J. Song
Cover Design	Marina Lee
Illustration	Jung-Yeon Choi
Design	Young-Ran Kwon
First Editor	Hye-Sung Seo
English Translator	Yoon-Jee Kim

Published	June 2013

UPC 8-84088-91742-5
ISBN 978-1-4803-5046-5

Completion Copyright of the text & musical examples © Korea Institute of Piano Pedagogy 2013
Illustration Copyright © Korea Institute of Piano Pedagogy 2013
International copyright secured. All rights reserved.

All rights reserved. No portion of this book may be reproduced, stored in a retrieval system,
or transmitted in any form or means- mechanical, photocopying, or other- without permission of KIPP publication.
Printed in Seoul, Korea

Contents

01 M. Clementi Op. 36 No. 1, 3rd movt. (p. 10)

02 M. Clementi Op. 36 No. 1, 1st movt. (p. 18)

03 Kuhlau Op. 55 No. 1, 1st movt. (p. 26)

04 Kuhlau Sonatine Op. 55 No. 1, 2nd movt. (p. 34)

05 M. Clementi Op. 36 No. 2, 1st movt. (p. 44)

06 M. Clementi Op. 36 No. 2, 3rd movt. (p. 52)

07 M. Clementi Op. 36 No. 3, 3rd movt. (p. 62)

08 M. Clementi Op. 36 No. 3, 1st movt. (p. 70)

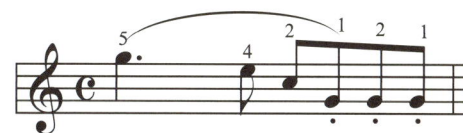

09 M. Clementi Op. 36 No. 4, 1st movt. (p. 78)

10 Kuhlau Op. 20 No. 1, 1st movt. (p. 86)

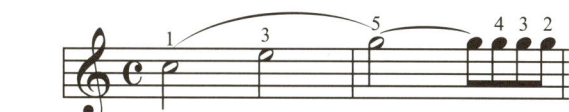

11 Kuhlau Op. 20 No. 1, 2nd movt. (p. 94)

12 Kuhlau Op. 20 No. 1, 3rd movt. (p. 100)

13 Kuhlau Op. 55 No. 2, 1st movt. (p. 112)

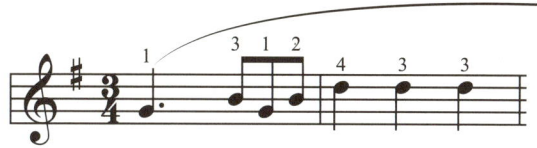

14 Kuhlau Op. 55 No. 2, 2nd movt. (p. 118)

What is an icon?

Here are friendly icons that will help you solve all of the riddles hidden in this book.
Befriend these smart icons, and you will soon become a brilliant pianist who can interpret and perform any challenging piece thrown at you.

Wecome to the Icon village!
Name those Icons!

What is an icon?

Icon is the best communicator.

Why ⏳ in the music?

If you see ⏳ on the computer screen, you can't do anything but wait, can you?

Pearl
A student who has studied scales with Ms. Silverplate.

Ms. Silverplate
A seasoned piano teacher who will help you resolve difficulties hidden in Sonatines.

※ Many of these icon stickers are explained in *Secrets to Scales Series* written by Joy Song.

Icons for Posture

Icon	Role	Explanation	Suggested Use
Shoulder down!	Keeps your shoulders down.	Whenever those sneaky shoulders go up without you knowing it, bring them down with this smart icon sticker.	p.21
The Turtle Shell	Helps form a firm hand shape and grip.	Palm like a turtle / Fingertips like hammers	p.36
The Bicep	Supports the thumb and the pinky to produce strong sounds.	This muscle must appear every time the thumb or the pinky must play.	p.40
The Protractor	Keeps the wrists and arms parallel to the keyboard.	Aligned with the keyboard / Wrist needs to move	p.29
Ms. Preview	Prepares eyes & hands for the notes that jump out.	Ms. Preview prevents mistakes. She may be the hardest worker of the Icon village! Refer to pages 60~61.	p.76
The Frog	Makes your wrist leap high.	Wrist jumps like on a pogo stick	p.36
	Makes your wrist squat before leaping. *Don't forget : You can't leap without squatting first!	This mascot squats on your lowered wrist and then leaps high to make your wrist higher. He will help you to produce beautiful sound. Refer to page 23.	Prepare with a lowered wrist. / Leap to make sound resonant.

Thumb Icons

"When you play a scale, the thumbs must move in the opposite direction."

"Thumb movement is tricky!"

Icon	Role	Explanation	Suggested Use
The Standing Thumb 	Helps produce healthy sound.	The thumb must always stand upright when melodies move fast. 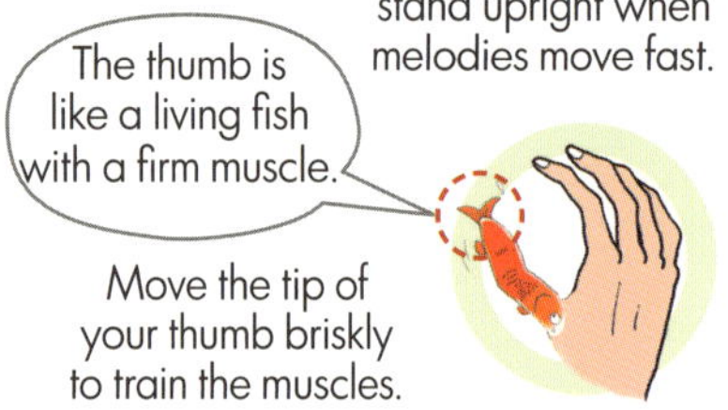 The thumb is like a living fish with a firm muscle. Move the tip of your thumb briskly to train the muscles.	p.20 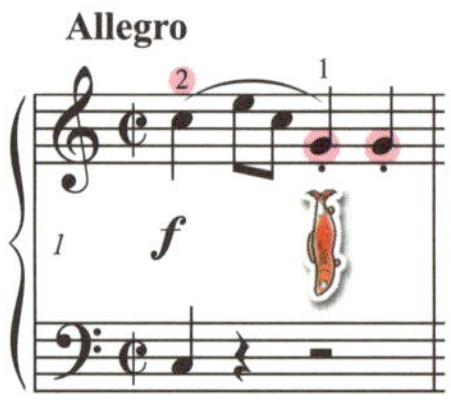 — Allegro
The Turning Fish  — Right thumb / Left thumb 	Indicates the direction to which the wrist must move.  "The fish escaped from the fish tank recently to watch over those whose wrists become sluggish when the thumb begins to play."	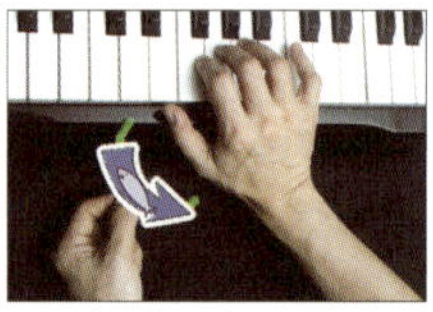 The right thumb to the right.  / The left thumb to the left.	p.80  — Con spirito / p.80 

Musical Icons
Icons for Musical Expression

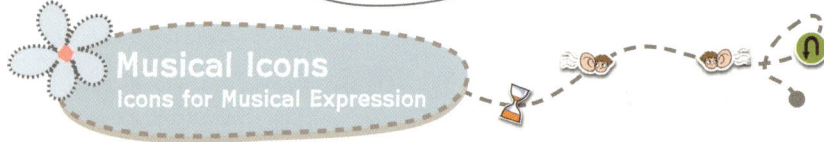

Icon	Role	Explanation	Suggested Use
The Hourglass 	Shows up whenever you need to wait long enough on pauses or long notes.	Remember, pauses are also part of the music!	p.39 
After – sound 	Helps you to listen to how the sound fades.	After-sound guy will help you to sound more musical. Refer to pages 42~43.	p.72 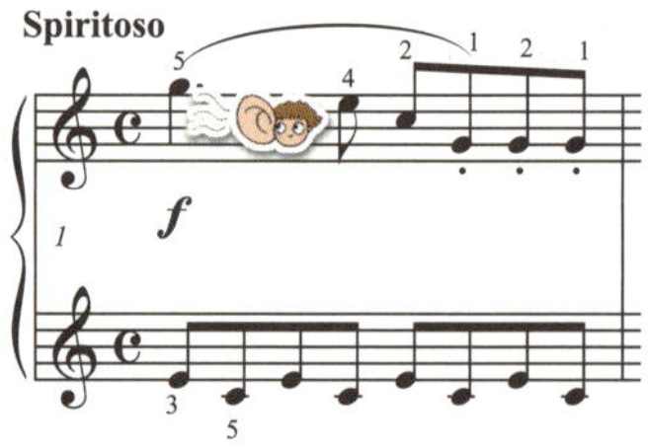 — Spiritoso
Before – sound 	Helps you to imagine the sound before the next note is to be played.	After-sound and Before-sound will create beautiful bridges between sections.	p.74 
The U-Turn 	Play softer when you turn around. When the notes up and down, there has to be a natural increase and decrease in volume.	 Does a car speed up when making a u-turn? No, it has to slow down. Decreasing speed means soft playing, just as a car driving upwards and downwards will have to speed down and up.	p.66  / p.36 

Icons for Interpretation

Icon	Role	Explanation	Suggested Use
Sticky	Applies the feeling of stickiness when chromatics show up.	You know how it feels when you step on a gum? It feels wonderfully sticky.	p.37
Melody Line	Helps with voicing the lines.	Bring out the outer lines (soprano and bass) clearly, and let the inner lines (alto and tenor) fill the space inside softly.	p.75
The Butterfly	Gives elegant dynamic nuances.	Whenever you have to use the wrist more, feel free and flutter like a butterfly.	p.46
Balance R>L L>R	Melody > Accompaniment	When the accompaniment becomes thicker, it will always disturb the melody. This icon controls the sound proportion between the melody and the accompaniment.	p.12
Sequence	Helps create a beautiful curve as the notes move up and down.	With the help of this icon, express the melodic movement as if a ribbon flutters. Refer to pages 24~25.	p.28
The Dynamics ① ② ③	Layers the different dynamic levels.	These three numberings help organize repeated melodies by stepwise dynamic levels.	p.47
Nuance	Expands or decreases sound. Attention: I express nuances subtler than simple crescendo and diminuendo.	Without this dandy icon, your playing will become dull. A seemingly invisible yet sophisticated icon that helps express musical nuances. Refer to page 98.	p.81

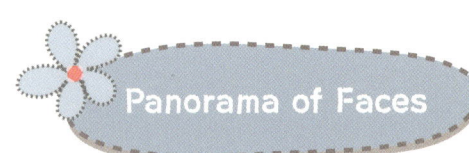

Panorama of Faces

Pearl's face changes whenever special harmonies show up. Refer to pages 32~33.

Icon	Meaning	Suggested Use
Dissonant	Pearl is uncomfortable because of a dissonant harmony.	p.29
Not resolved	Pearl is dissatisfied because something hasn't resolved yet.	p.72
Transition harmony	No final resolution took place, but Pearl is still a bit relieved.	p.76
Solution / Tonic	Pearl is completely satisfied after having reached the goal.	p.13
Minor / Sad	Pearl is touched and has tears in her eyes.	p.75
sf (sforzando) / sudden forte	Pearl is trying to make an important point.	p.13

You may agree or not agree with the meaning of icons here, but you can use them whichever way you feel. Icons are just tools to remind you of all the musical & technical expressions.

How about creating your own icon?

Preface

*"Why does following all the markings on the score
still lead to unsophisticated playing?"*

*"Shouldn't students be able to create their own interpretations
without the help of actual lessons?"*

With these questions in mind, I began to teach Sonatines to piano teachers in master classes at KIPP. Since its inception, the master classes have produced countless competition prize winners. What's more amazing is that, through these classes, students began to acquire abilities in interpreting more advanced repertoire like Mozart, Haydn and Beethoven.

I always question myself whenever I start to write a book like this one.

Why is this book needed?
Why am I once again embarking upon this difficult journey?

I would never have started this process if I were going to include superficial and unspecific instructions. My desire to teach students how to catch a fish instead of catching it for them and to make the learning process fun for everyone has not wavered through all these years, and it is what still drives me to work long nights.

Turning real-life lessons into lessons in print leads to limitations. I hoped to minimize these limitations by using icons and distinctive language, that are easily understandable for those who are familiar with my other best-selling books *Scale Secrets* and the *Nine Gifts from a Piano Teacher* (which are also currently being translated into English). For this new English version of Sonatine Secrets, I added detailed explanations with sample excerpts of the Sonatines.

I thank all of my wonderful colleagues who have joined me on this lonely path: Hye Seung Seo, who first helped me to record and organize all of my lessons and gave me the idea for this project, Young-Ran Kwon, who has so crisply cleared up all of the complicated edits, Yoon-Jee Kim, who has translated into English, Helen Kim, the vice director of KIPP, and the teachers at Song's Music School, who have devoted their lives to KIPP. Without Jennifer Lynn's empowering heart and practical help, I would not have had the courage to publish the English version. I also thank my dear friend Dr. Pam Jones, who was in the same class with me under Johana Harris at UCLA. She has supported me and believed that my idea of piano teaching has to be translated into English.

I always owe my musical children Esther, Joanna, John, Tim and my wonderfully analytical husband, who always helps me to realize my dreams and is awake with me until very late into the night as I type and revise endlessly.

Finally, I give all of my glory to the Lord, who is the ultimate source of my ideas, wisdom and inspiration.

2013 in Beverly Hills, CA
Joy Jeehai Song

M. Clementi Sonatine

Op. 36 No. 1, 3rd Movement

Ms. Silverplate's Smart Tips

🌼 **Please take a look at my 3rd and 4th fingers. They always get tangled up!**

Level 1   Let's play slowly.

Feel the 🔴 and maintain the 🐢 !! Also, keep the palm firm!

Level 2   Now, faster!

🐸🐸 on the first note, and think of one measure as one beat.

🌼 **Scales are everywhere. How do I make them expressive?**

For longer scales, find out what key they are in.

Level 1   Mission: find that scale!

Find the beginning and the end of the G Major scale, and divide it.
Isn't it now easier to practice the scale?

Level 2   Add nuances!

Play each of the three scales in its own distinct way.
Then what is created is wonderfully nuanced musicality.

Ms. Silverplate's Lesson Overview:

What is important in this piece is the contrast between *p* in mm. 1 ~ 8 and *f* in mm. 9 ~ 16. Here, it is hard to bring out the *f*. To make the contrast, try to play the *f* in m. 9 as loudly as possible, and then choose the volume of the *p* accordingly. This will produce an effective contrast.

M. Clementi Op. 36 No. 1, 3rd movt.

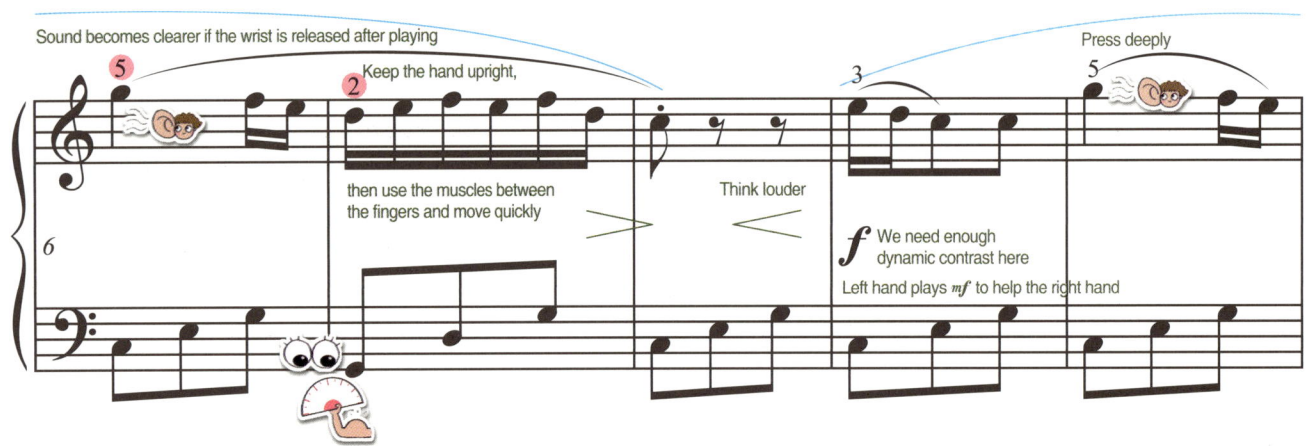

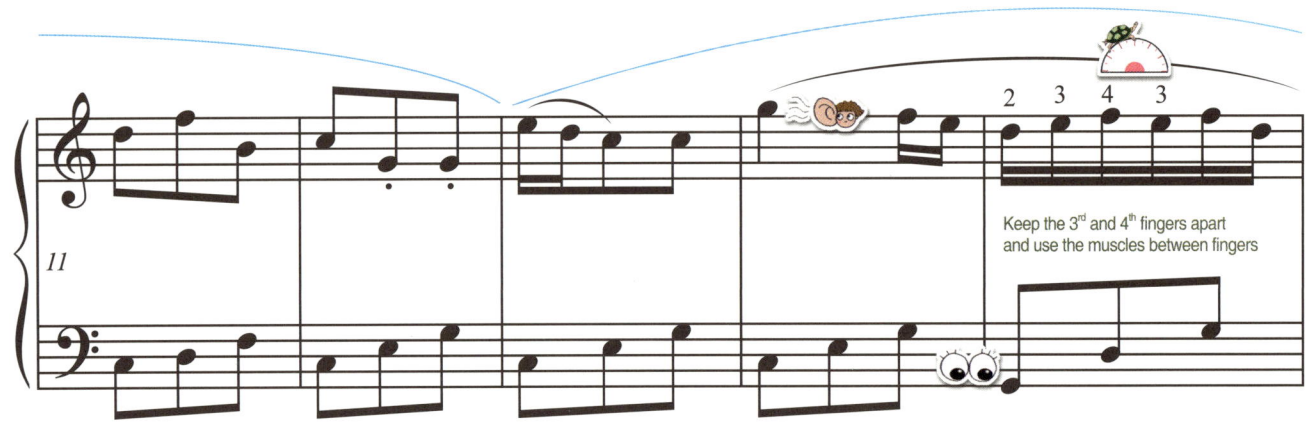

B
16
Firm fingertips
p
Gently touch with fingertip
Much softer than the melody
f
In fast tempo, keep the thumb firm and upright, and bounce it (Control by listening to the melody in the right hand)
Feel the harmonic change per measure
21
The descending G Major scale
p
Show harmonic color change
f
A sudden f
The left hand should also get actively bigger - that will liven up the f
26
The wrist should not be too high or too low
Show the nuance of the descending G Major scale
31
dim.
Feel the rests - they also require concentration
p
pp
Soft sound should be played only with fingertips and with round and firm hand
Play the accompaniment softly! React to the F and D in the right hand

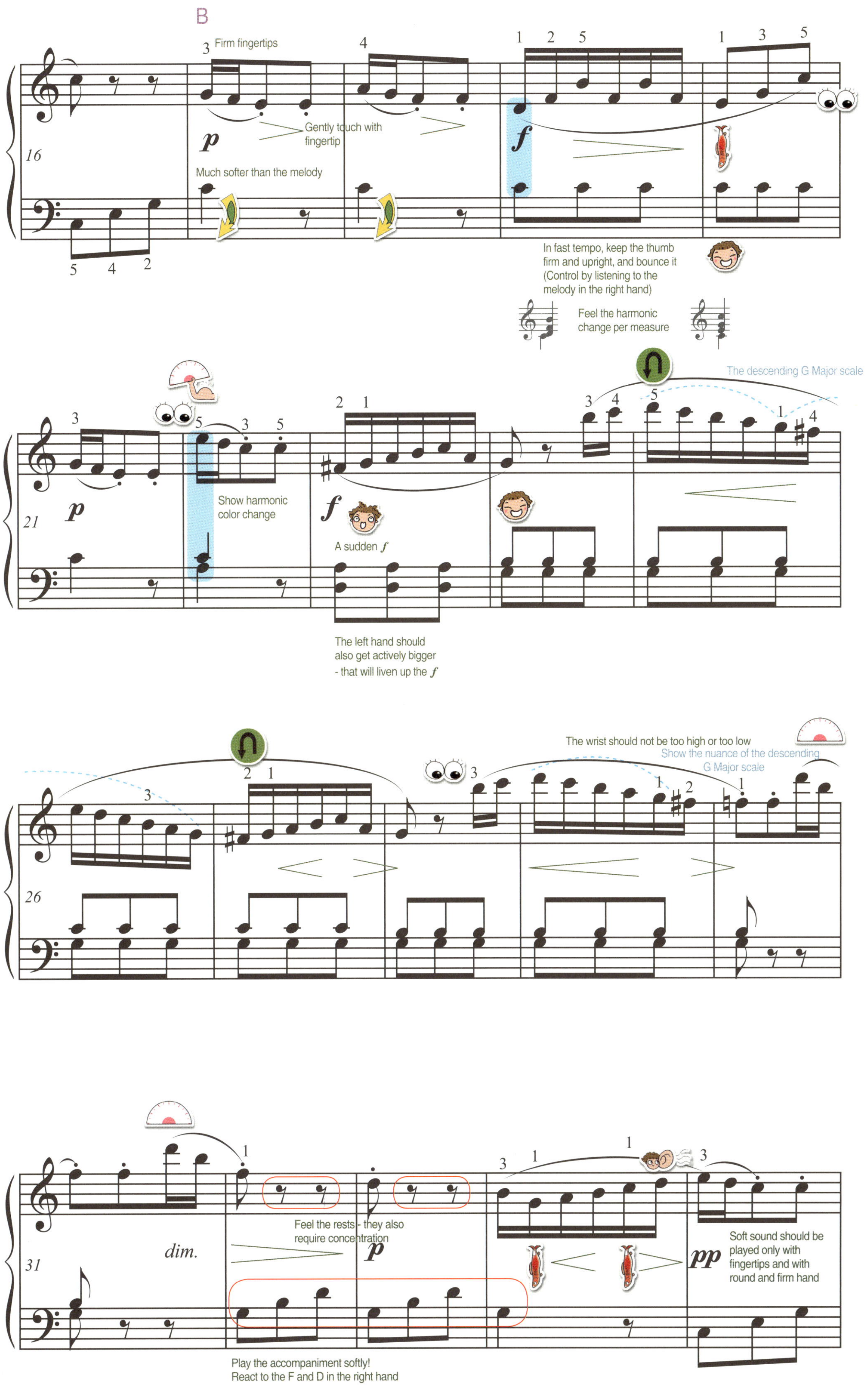

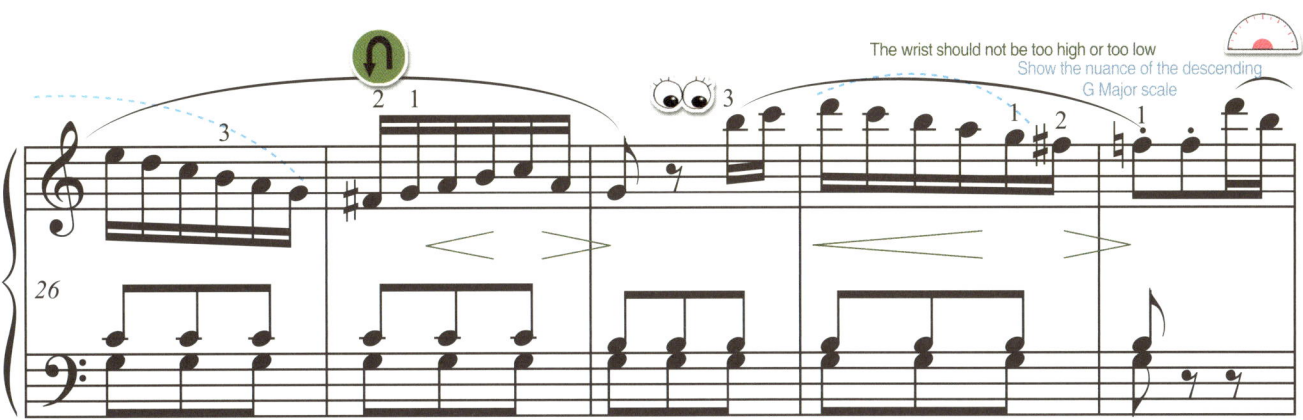

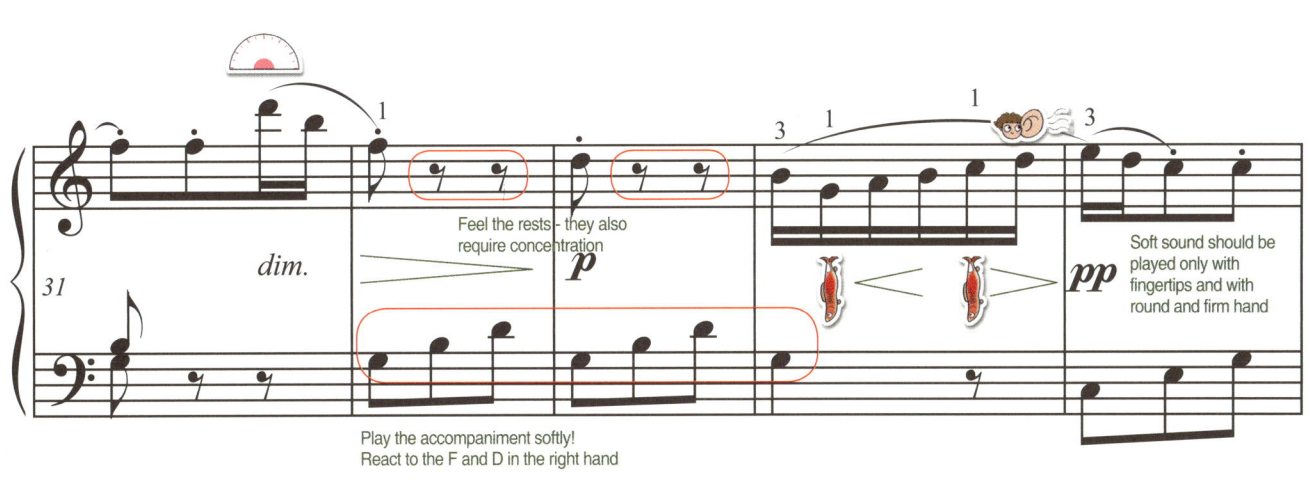

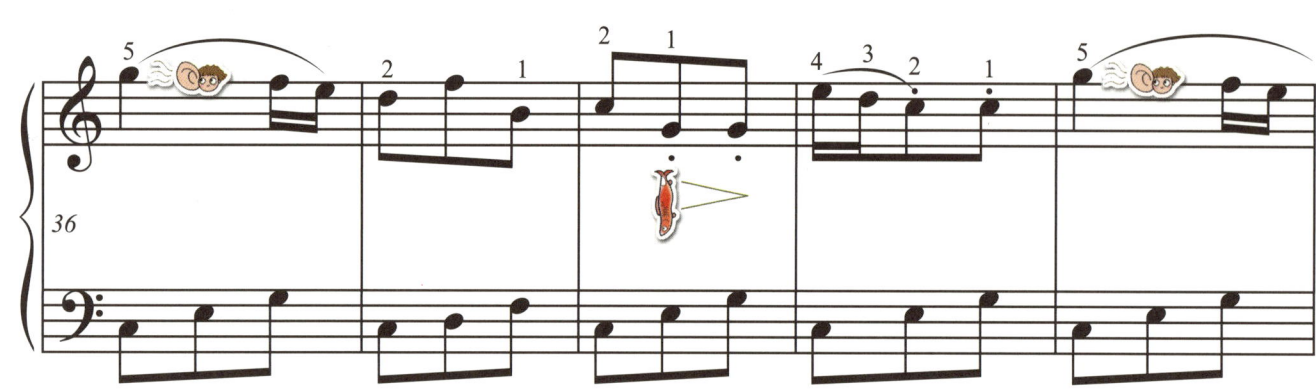
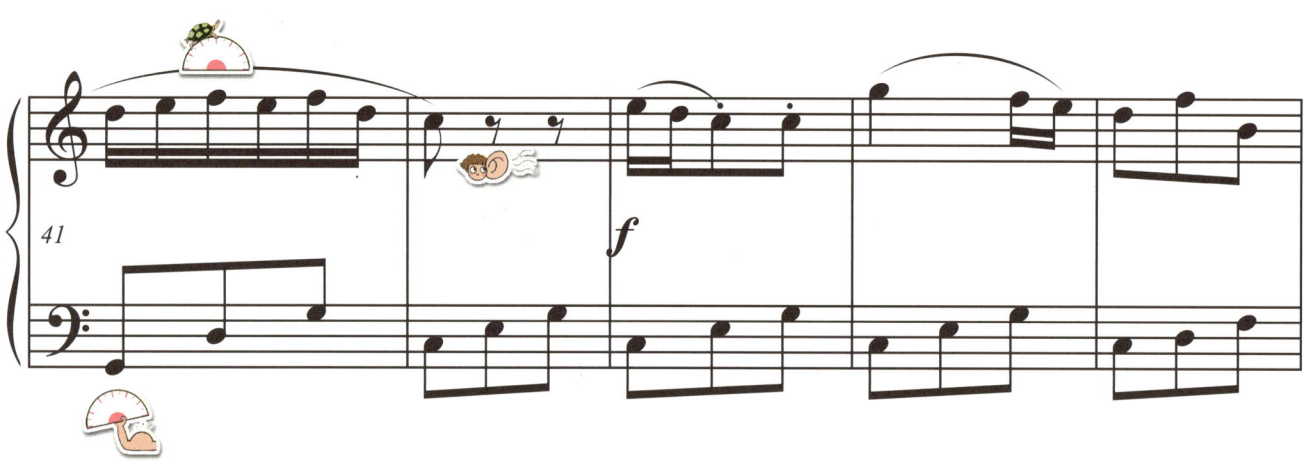

The Coda

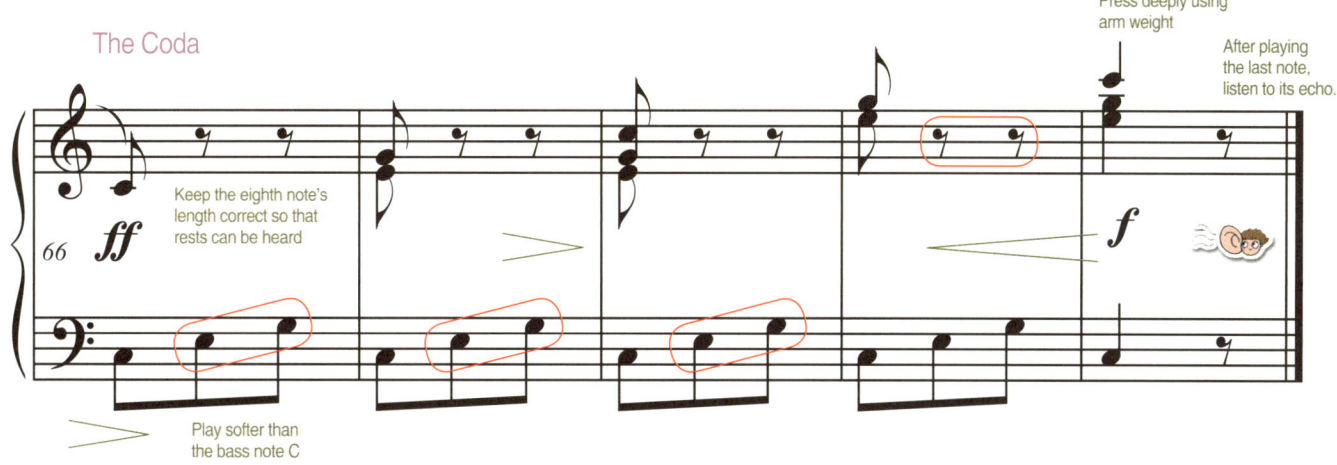

Sonatine **Story**

Hello, my friends!
Now that you've begun working with Sonatine Secrets, your sound should have already become louder than before, and your fingers more fluent than ever.
But your fingers alone can't make music sound beautiful, if you don't think about the dynamics. I will now tell you the secret to playing beautifully and brilliantly.
If you follow along and learn one new thing at a time, you will soon become an excellent performer!

❀ How to make an elegant crescendo?

Colorful contrast between forte and piano makes music sound magnificent.
Crescendo is one of the ways to make this contrast effective.
Do you know the secret behind making an elegant crescendo?
If you just keep getting louder whenever you see cresendo, you'll just sound crude. So, what should you do?
Try to make the last note of the crescendo softer, even if it doesn't say so in the music.
The melody will then become graceful.

One more thing: if two repeated notes at the end of a figure both have staccatos on them,
playing them equally loud would make them sound harsh. Instead, play the last note softly.
Also, try bouncing your wrists gently. Keep these things in mind!

M. Clementi Op. 36 No. 2, Movt. III

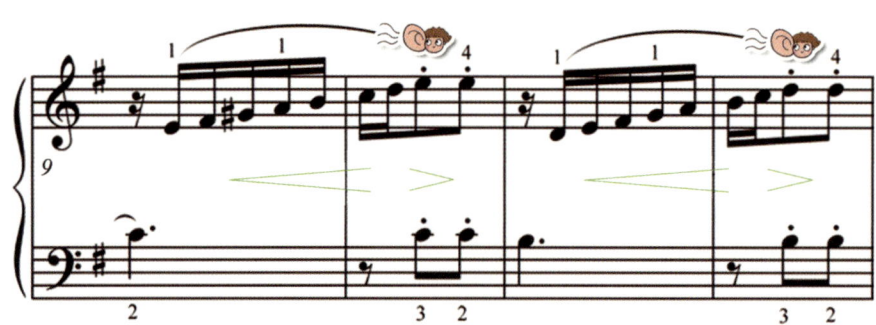

Where is *f*'s real home?

Why does music sound unsophisticated even when we follow the markings in the music faithfully?

The reason is that when we follow the music, we end up playing either too loudly or too softly.

Let's not make *f* so loud so suddenly.

We have to consider the phrasing and arrive at *f* more gradually.

Only then will *f* become sophisticated.

"You wanna know something?

The place *f* really belongs is actually a little farther beyond where it is marked."

Kuhlau Op. 55 No. 1, Movt. I

M. Clementi Sonatine

Op. 36 No. 1 in C Major, 1st Movement

Ms. Silverplate's Smart Tips

🌼 How can I show the difference between *f* and *p* effectively?

Try to listen to the reverberation of the first four measures in *f*

○ Try playing the *f* as powerfully as you can.
  p will sound much more effective if *f* is loud enough.

○ Play the *p* from m. 5 **within the echo** of the previous *f* section.
  But be careful! Don't lose the strength of your fingertips when the sound should be softer.
  The softer tone also should be intensive as well.

🌼 The tempo gets slower because my hands are too small for the octave leaps!

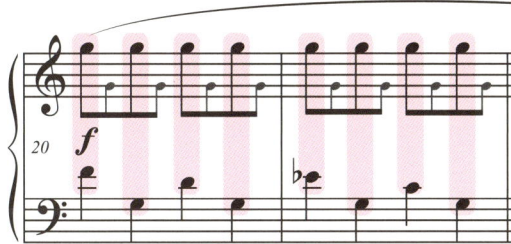

○ Try playing only the highlighted notes of both hands!
  Your rhythm will become more precise just by imagining the bottom note (G) in the octaves.

○ Is there a way to make it sound musical as well?
  Listen to the sound of the top G, and try mixing in the bottom G discreetly.
  (If you want to hide the clumsiness of the right hand, just emphasize the quarter-note beats.)

Is it better now? You just need agile arms and sensitive ears.

M. Clementi Op. 36 No. 1, 1st movt.

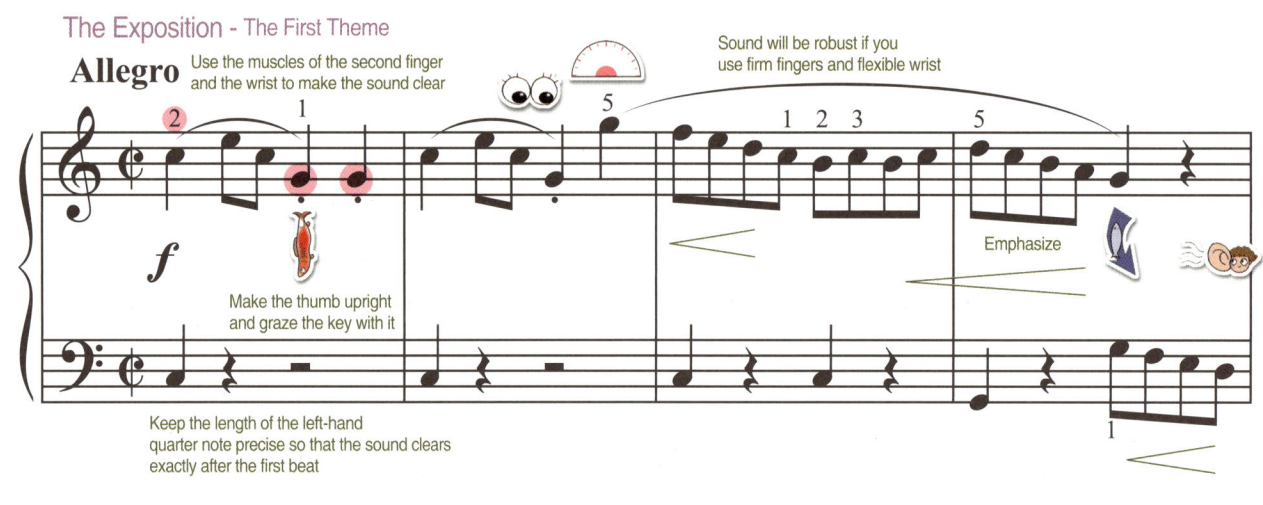
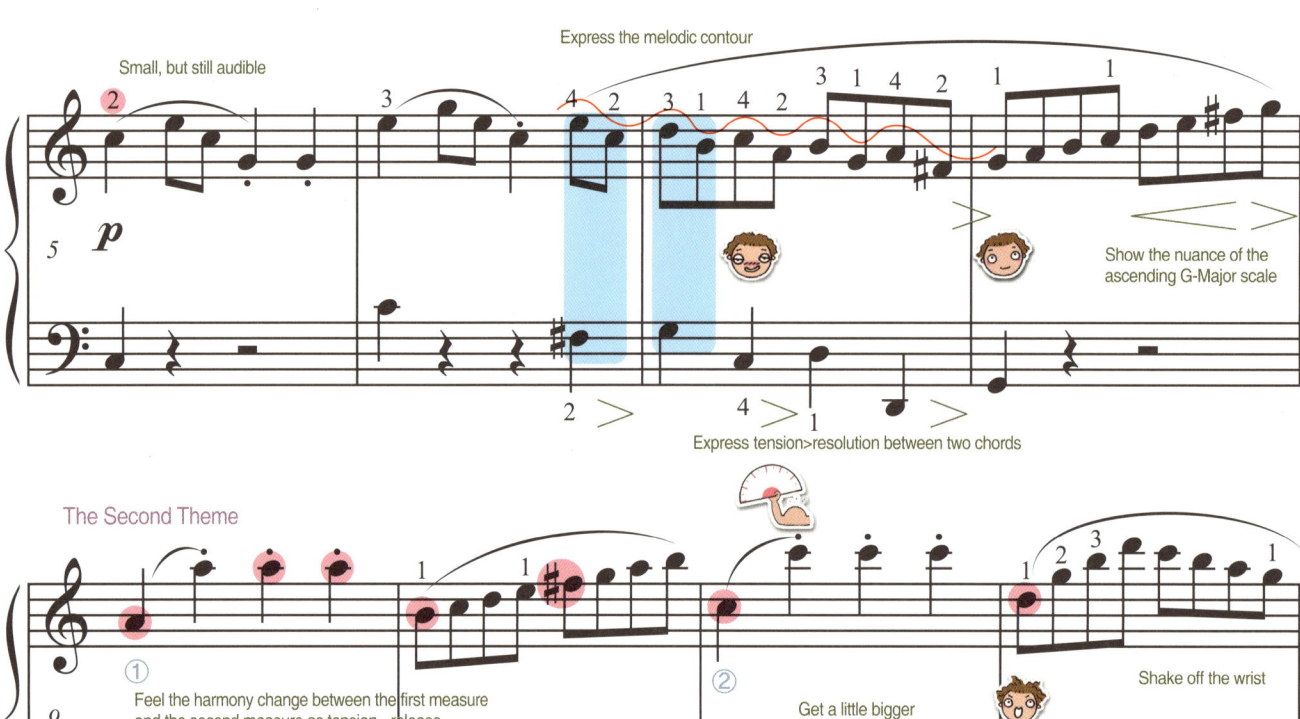

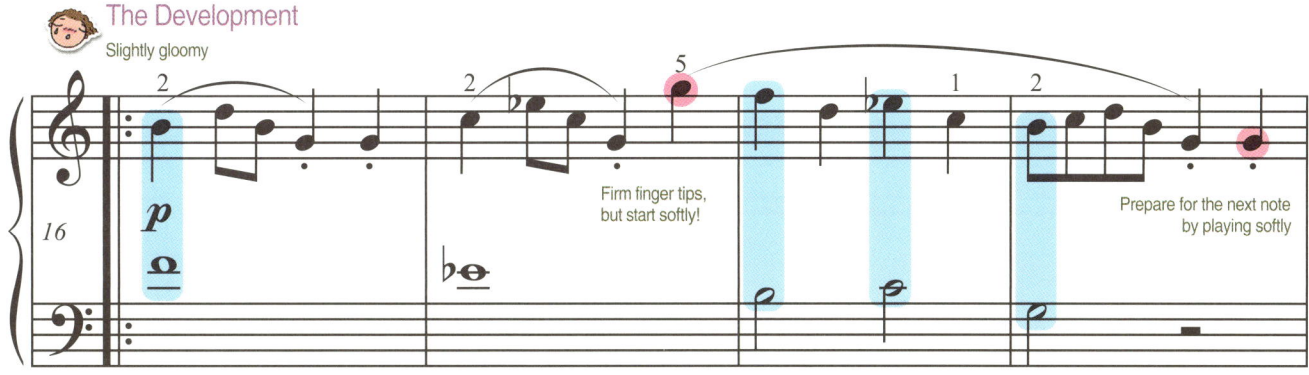
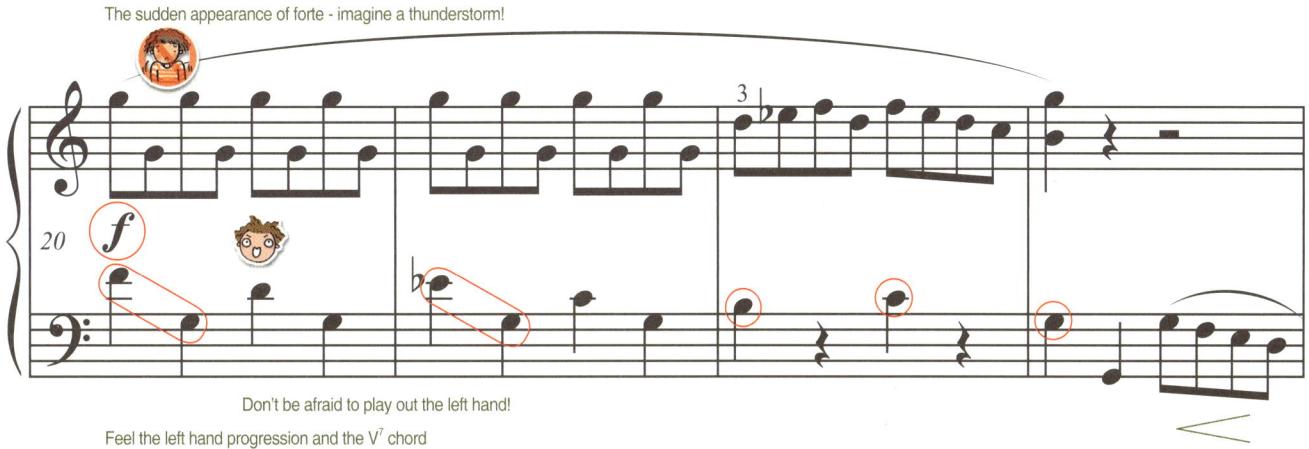

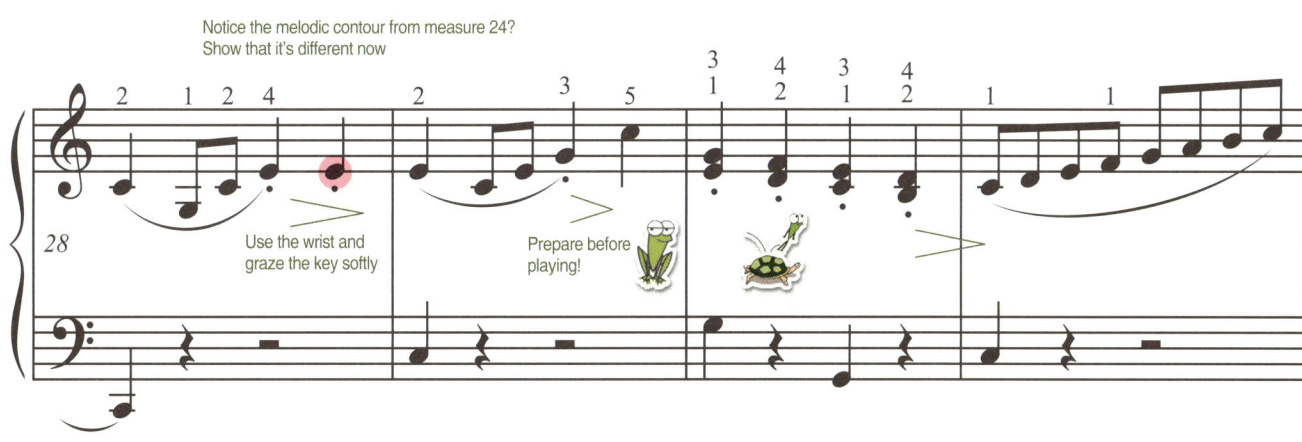

The Second Theme

The chord progresses — Feel the flow of the right hand ascending until the top G

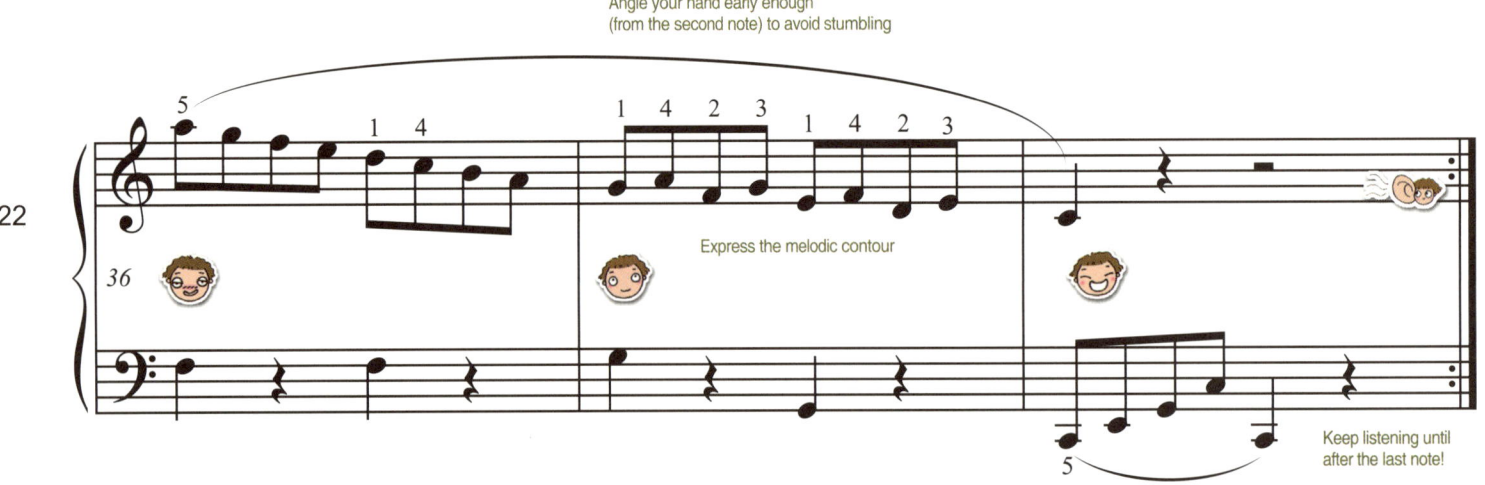

Angle your hand early enough (from the second note) to avoid stumbling

Express the melodic contour

Keep listening until after the last note!

Have you become friends with the icons from the Icon village?

Your icon friends are this book's special feature.

They will appear (sometimes many of them at once!)

To help you figure out how to play better.

You've already met some of them, like the Protractor

- which will help your fifth finger to stay parallel to the keys,

and the Turtle Shell - which will help you play more clearly.

Don't forget to keep watching out for their help!

The Frog icon has something to say. :)

When I appear, you know that you should keep your wrist down

and then bring it up.

I noticed that many of you keep bringing the wrist up

without remembering to bring it down beforehand,

so your wrist keeps getting higher and higher!

Don't forget that the downward motion should always

come before the upward motion!

Down and up! Up and down! We are a pair!

Sonatine **Story**

Introducing *Ms. Sequence*
– the world champion who shakes up melodies like a ribbon gymnast shaking up ribbons!

Have you heard of a "sequence"? It sounds scary, but it's actually simple.
A melodic pattern that repeats over and over - that's basically it.
Sequences appear often especially in Bach's Inventions.
Let's explore in detail the spell-binding work of *Ms. Sequence*!

Ms. Sequence

❋ How should I play those various sequences?

Kuhlau Op. 55 No. 1, Movt. I

M. Clementi Op. 36 No. 4, Movt. I

Kuhlau Op. 20 No. 1, Movt. III

01 **Observe the patterns.**
   Actively show that the notes go up and down.

02 **Play every note firmly.**
   With firm fingertips, pull on the keys from your knuckles (Refer to "Sonatine Story" on p.122).
   Your palm has to be firm, but the wrist has to be elastic.

03 **Group each pattern and pluck at the first notes.** (if the first note is the strong beat)
   When you can play every note solidly,
   group the notes into units and slightly pluck with a bouncing
   wrist at the first notes.

04 **Insert nuances/intonation.**
   Get slightly bigger and softer within each pattern,
   just like our speech naturally fluctuates in pitch.

❦ Sequences show up in these places!

1. When it acts as a bridge between one theme and another.

   Kuhlau Op. 20 No. 3, Movt. III

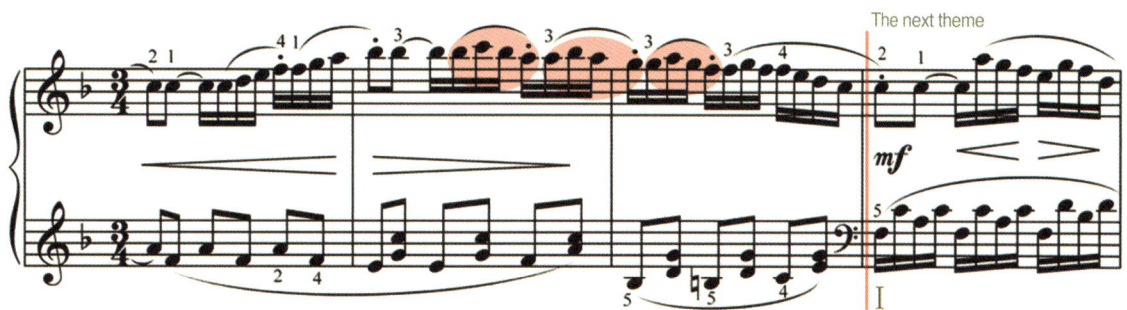

2. When it's trying to spice things up - an arpeggio sequence is particularly brilliant.
   Use the wrist and the arm together in these places!

   M. Clementi Op. 36 No. 3, Movt. III

3. When it hightens the atmosphere to reach a climax.

   M. Clementi Op. 36 No. 4, Movt. I

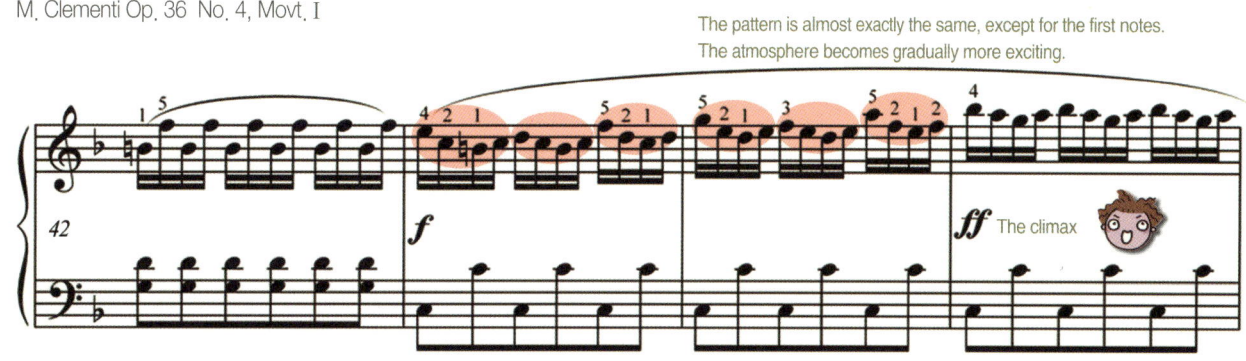

Kuhlau Sonatine

Op. 55 No. 1 in C Major, 1st Movement

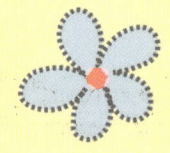

> # Ms. Silverplate's Smart Tips

❀ **The accompaniment keeps getting louder without me knowing it.
What should I do?**

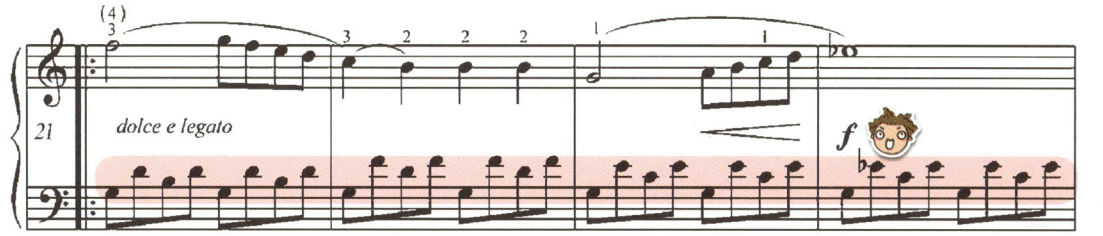

Put some weight on your fingertips and crawl on the keys with them like a cat taking stealthy steps with its paws.
Go slowly enough into the keys to make a softer sound. It's hard at first,
but once you get used to it, it's the fastest way to achieve soft sound.

◉ First, practice playing each note of the melody securely.

The melody must win over the left hand.

◉ Then try playing the left hand very softly.

If you're applying more strength on your left hand than before, that means it's going well.

◉ Show the color of the harmonies!

As you get to m. 24, make a crescendo with your left hand with the melody line.

It'll make the music more alive.

❀ **Use a strong grip and a flexible wrist for the staccato and legato chords!**

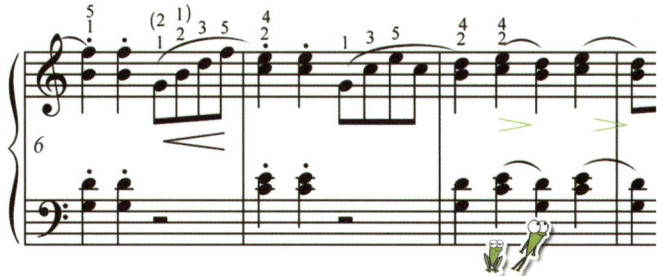

Legato chords are difficult even for skilled pianists.
But if you use the wrist, they will be a piece of cake.

◉ Before playing the chords, prepare with 🐢 + 🐸.

◉ As you play the chord, grip the keys and pull away.

Why don't you first try practicing gripping on the piano cover?

◉ On the second chord of the two-chord slur,

bring the wrist up rapidly like a frog leaping up.

As you bounce with your wrist, listen for the lingering echo of the note

after the release of the chord. 🐸 + 👂

Kuhlau Op.55 No.1, 1st movt.

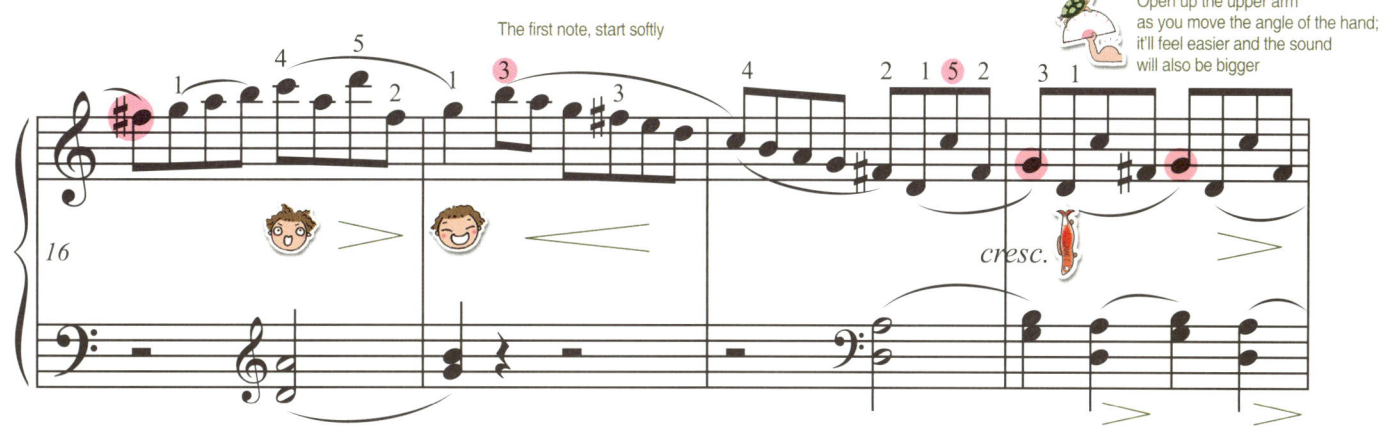
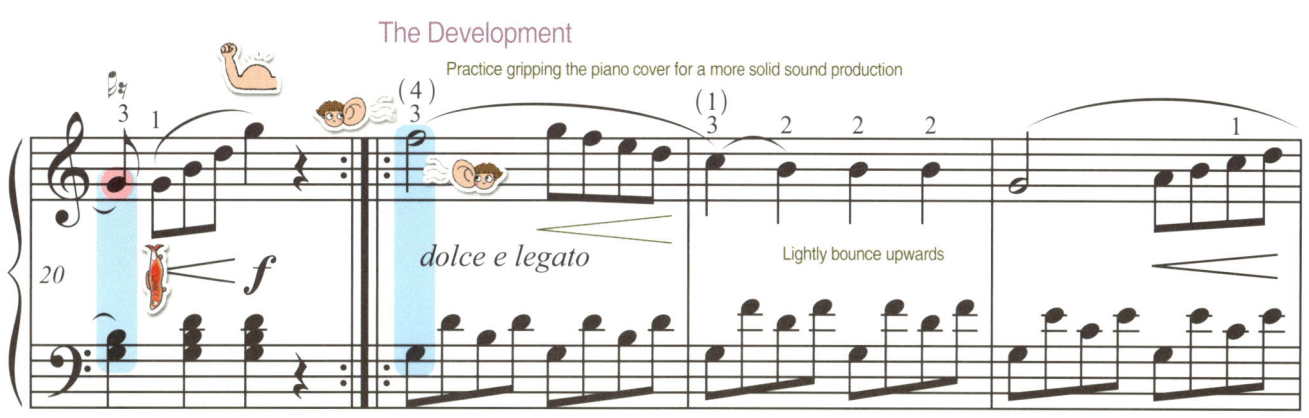
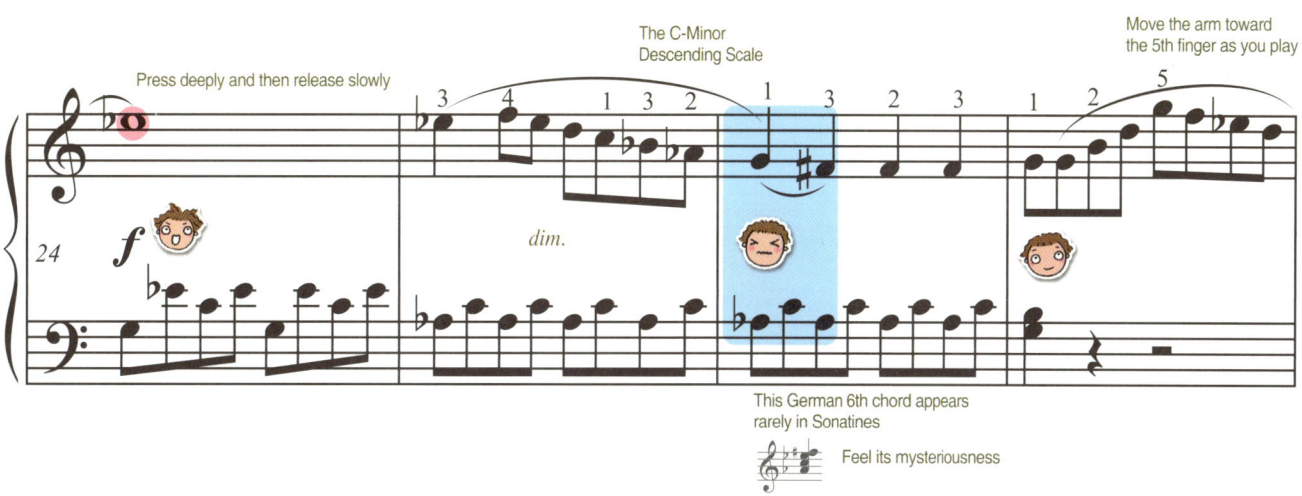

"The chord slurs in the right hand sound sluggish. What should I do?"

1. Try pinching firmly the first chord in the two-note slur.
2. Then bounce the wrist upward as you play the second chord in the slur.

Ms. Silverplate

The Second Theme

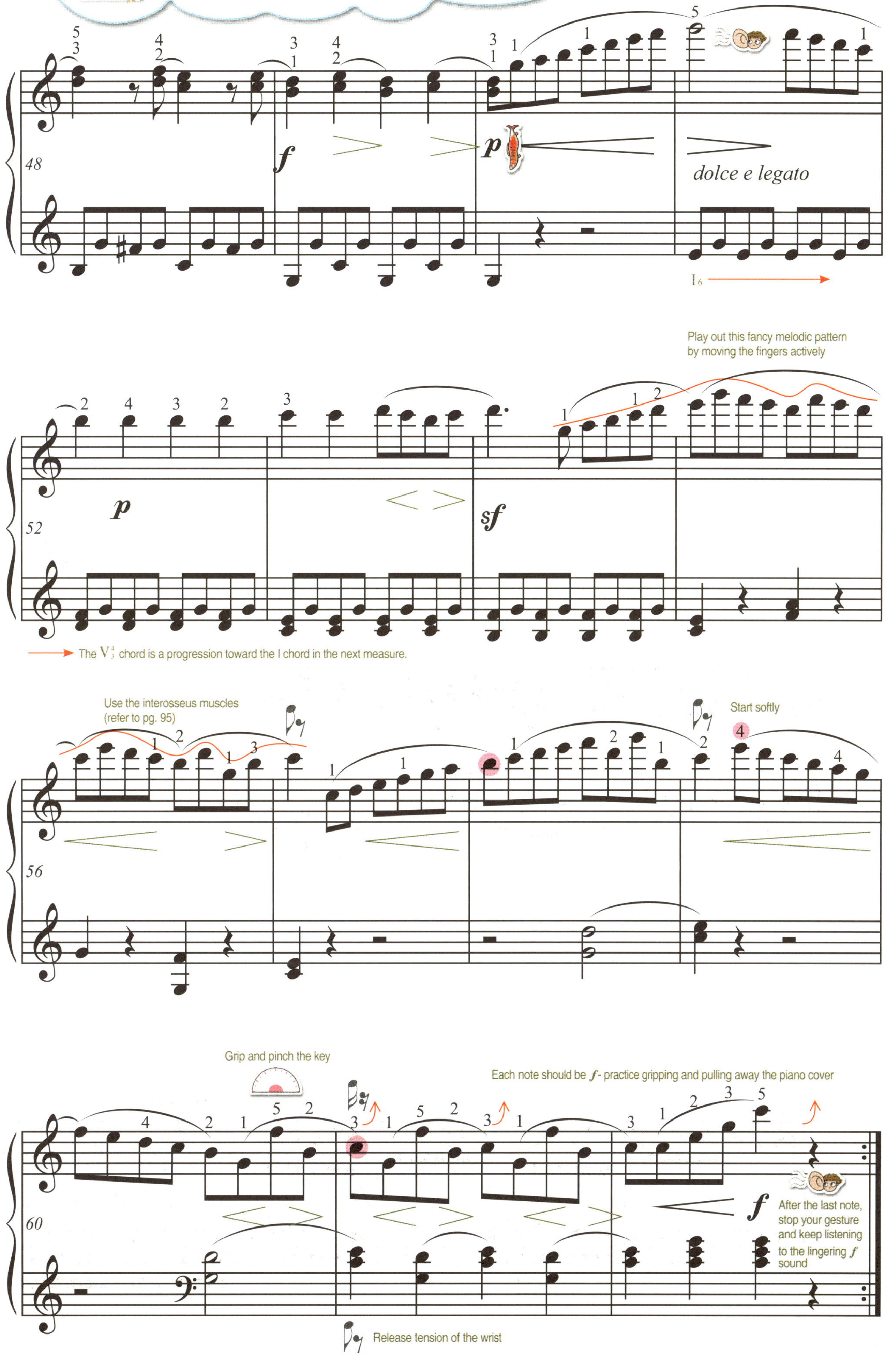

Sonatine Story

Look for the different facial expressions in a harmonic progression!

In this chapter, we'll take a look at the different colors and emotions harmonic progressions can display.
Think of a harmonic progression as a pathway that links one part of music with another.
This pathway plays an important role in making music sound either sophisticated or unsophisticated.
That's why composers must always work hard to think of harmonic progressions.

 Remember 2 things if you want to play harmonic progressions more musically!

1. Pinpoint chords that are more unusual or have accidentals and show them.
2. When you emphasize one chord, listen for its aftersound
   and then play the next chord (resolution) a bit softer.

❀ Time for some warm-up! Practicing tension〉release!

M. Clementi Op. 36 No. 3, Movt. I

For the tension〉release between two chords,
listen for the echo of the first chord and then play the next chord softer.

❀ Find that dissonance!

M. Clementi Op. 36 No. 2, Movt. III

Sonatine Story

❀ The bewitching diminished-7th! Let's show it off!

M. Clementi Op. 36 No. 2, Movt. I

Try to be lyrical and bring out the F in the right hand. Then enjoy the note.

❀ Expose those dissonant neighbor-tones!

Kuhlau Op. 20 No. 1, Movt. III

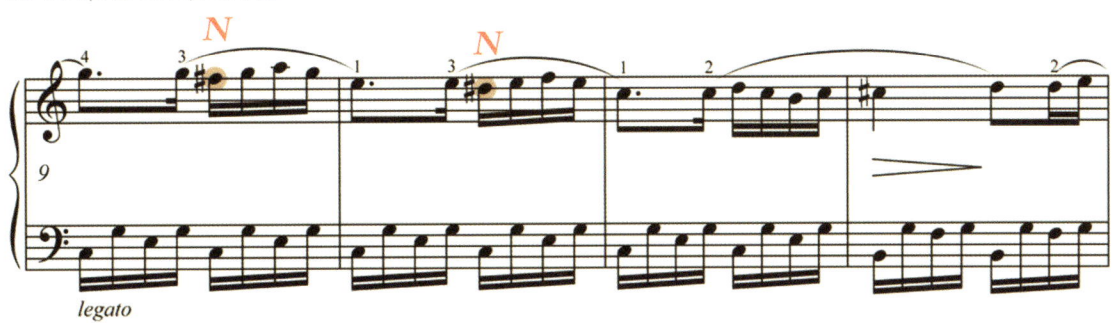

The melody feels dissonant because of the chromatic-tones.
Don't bring them out, but listen for them and just go on discreetly.

(*N* : Neighboring-tone is a note that is a step higher or lower than a note.
It is a non-harmonic tone that is often dissonant.)

Kuhlau Op. 55 No. 1, Movt. I

In Minor, there will be more chords that are unusual and therefore worth emphasizing.

Kuhlau Sonatine

Op. 55 No. 1 in C Major, 2nd Movement

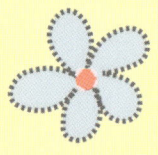

Ms. Silverplate's Smart Tips

❀ **I keep stumbling in those intimidating chromatic scales. What should I do?**

- Look at the right hand. It looks complicated, but it's only a chromatic scale, isn't it?
  You don't even have to read the notes if you can figure out the pattern.
  Fingering of a chromatic scale is so easy. It is illustrated in another one of my book, *Secret to Scale*.

- If you want both hands to play exactly together, try playing the highlighted chords first.

- Next, play as written, but think of each measure as a group.
  Bounce on the first note of the chromatic run on each bar, and use the momentum to go further.

❀ **What can I do with fancy melodic sequences that go on and on?**

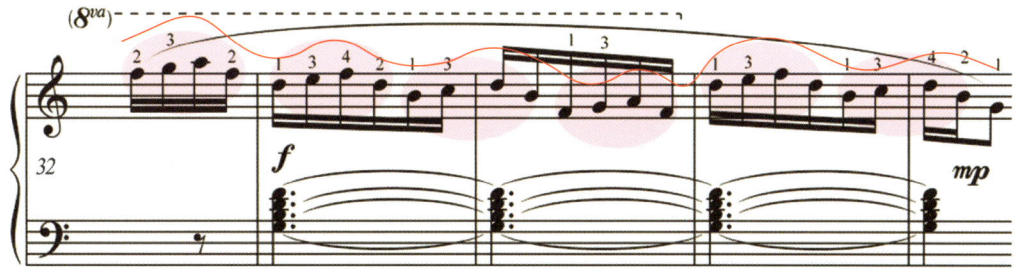

Ms. Sequence is quite fancy and appealing, isn't it? But it can trip you up.
Let's take a look carefully.

- First, group every four notes. You can surely see the pattern clearly.
  It's that world champion Ms. Sequence again!

- Next, observe carefully the ⌒ on your wrist and arm according to the fingering.

- If you also do a slight crescendo and diminuendo as you go up and down the pattern,
  it will sound much more sophisticated and beautiful.

Kuhlau Sonatine Op. 55 No. 1, 2nd movt.

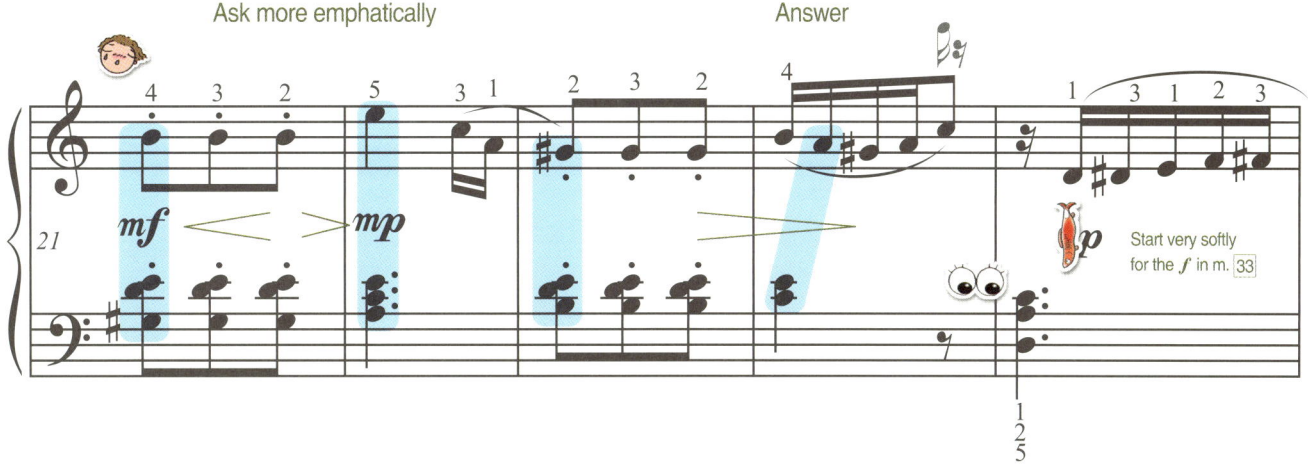

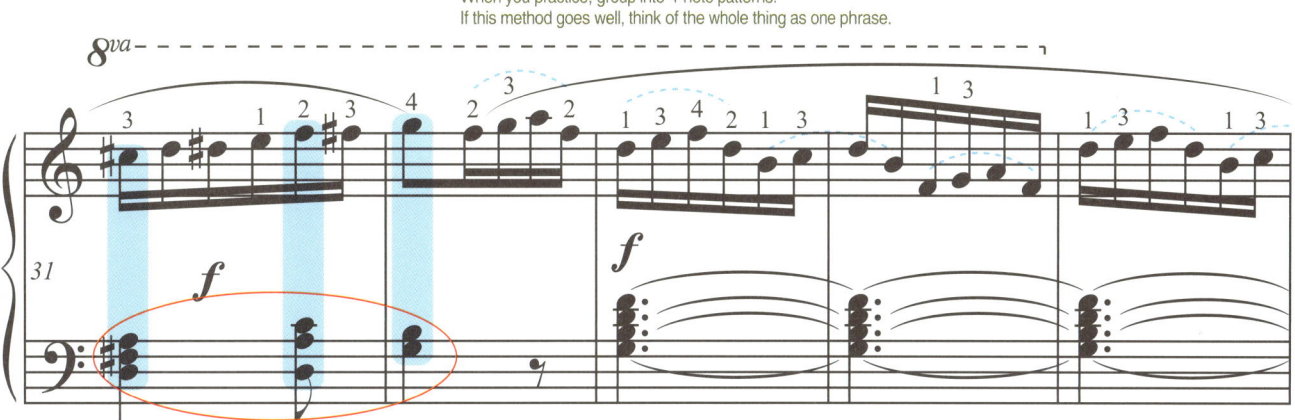
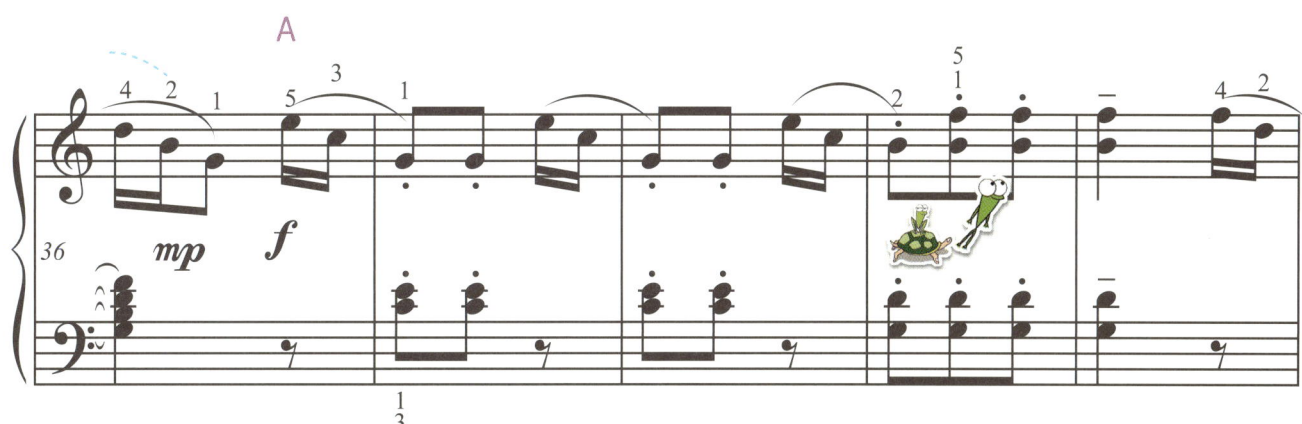

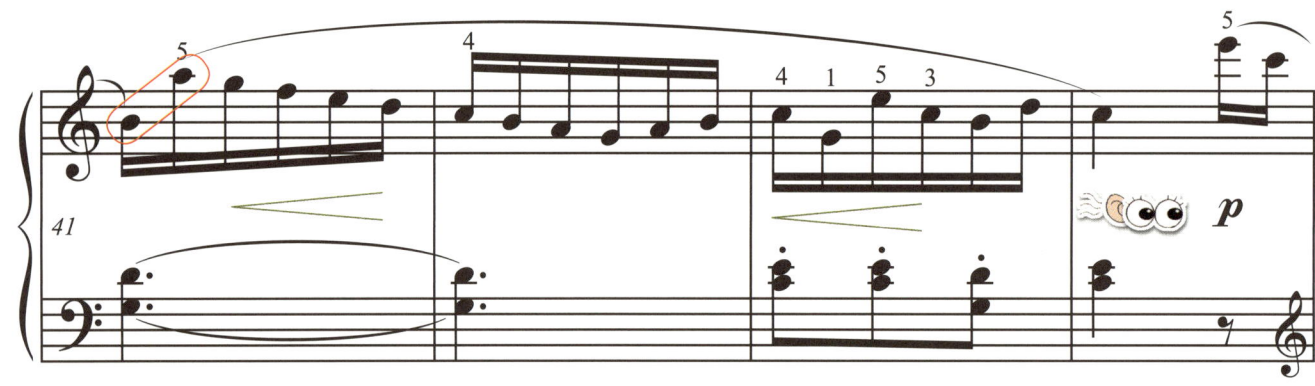

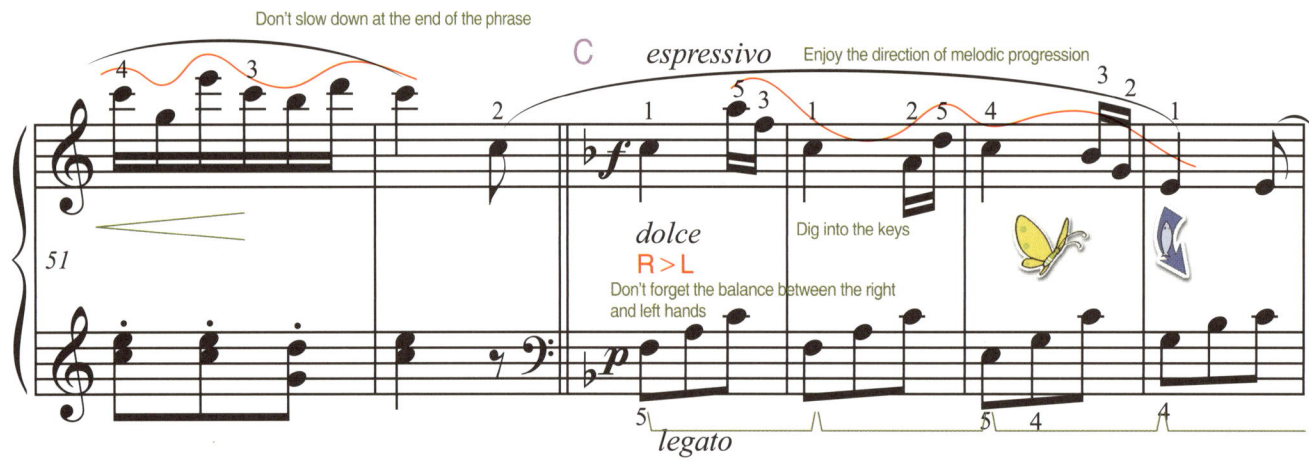
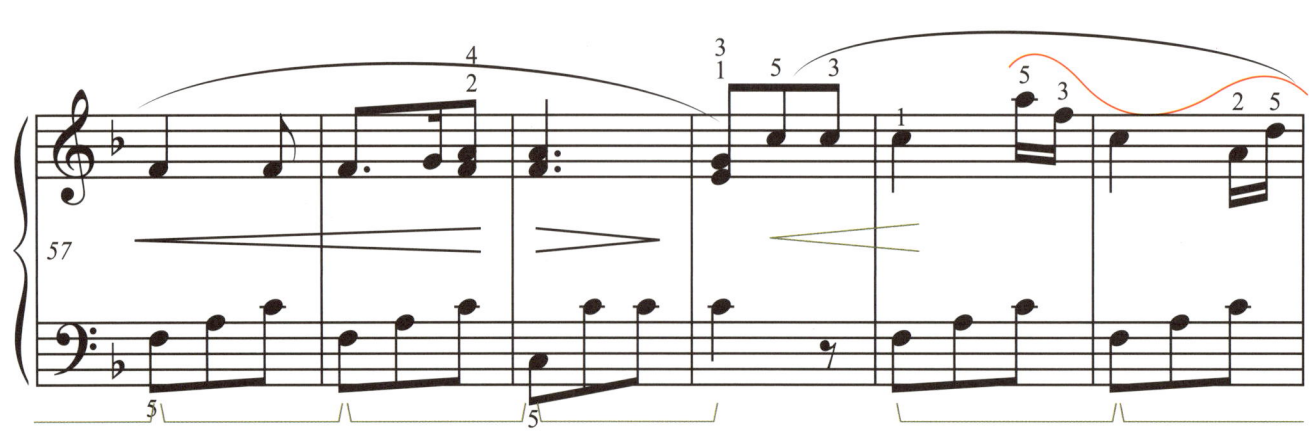

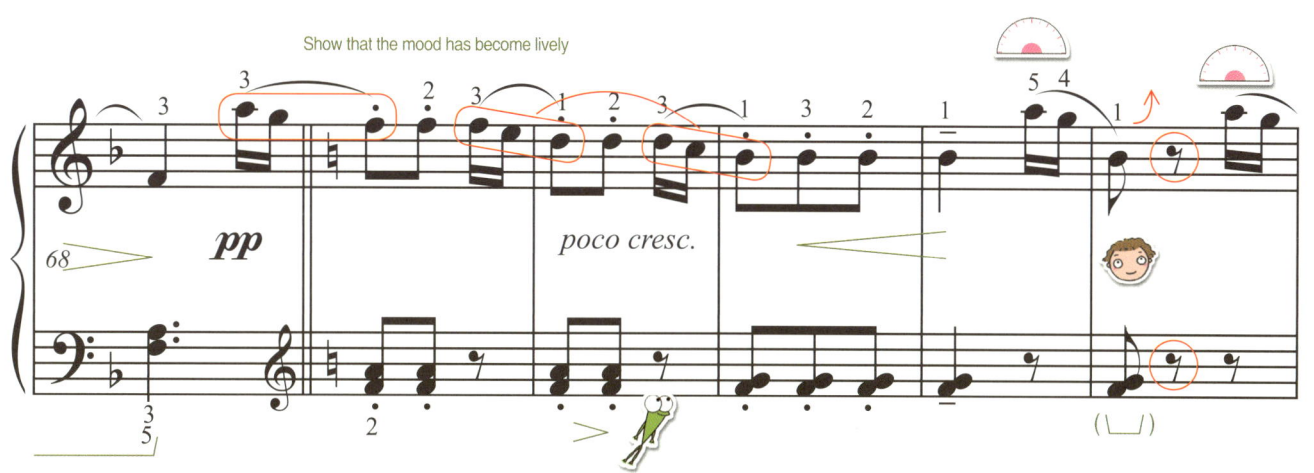

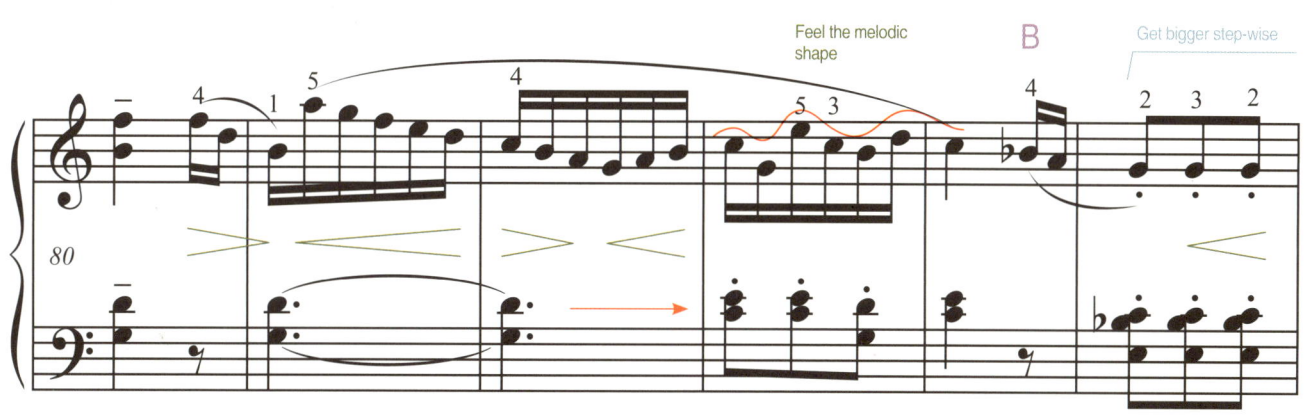

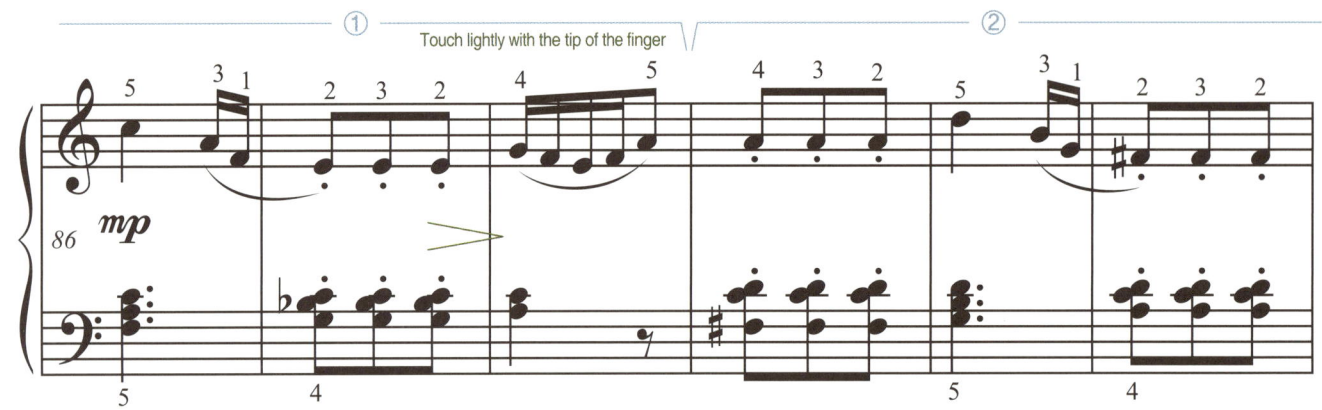
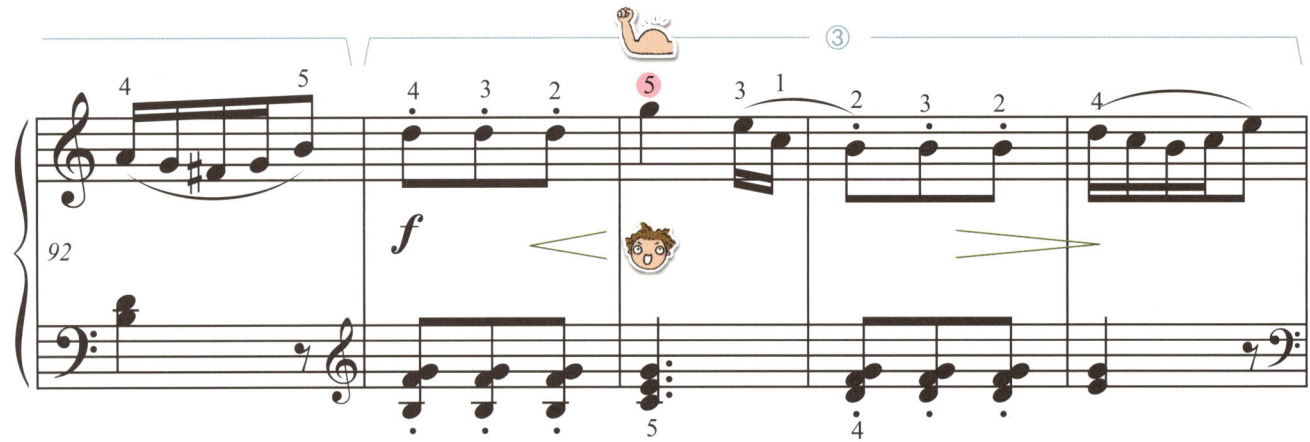

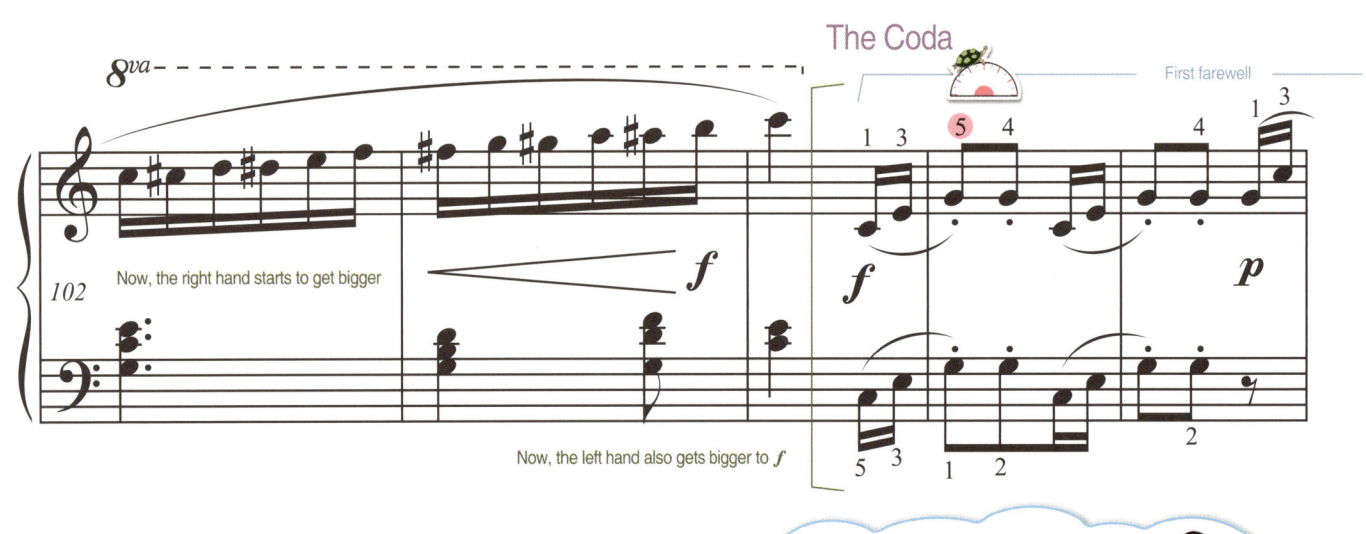

Just because you're going upward doesn't mean that you should do a crescendo!

If you're unsure of what to do, try singing the melody line. If you play the high E softly and then make a crescendo, it will sound more musical.

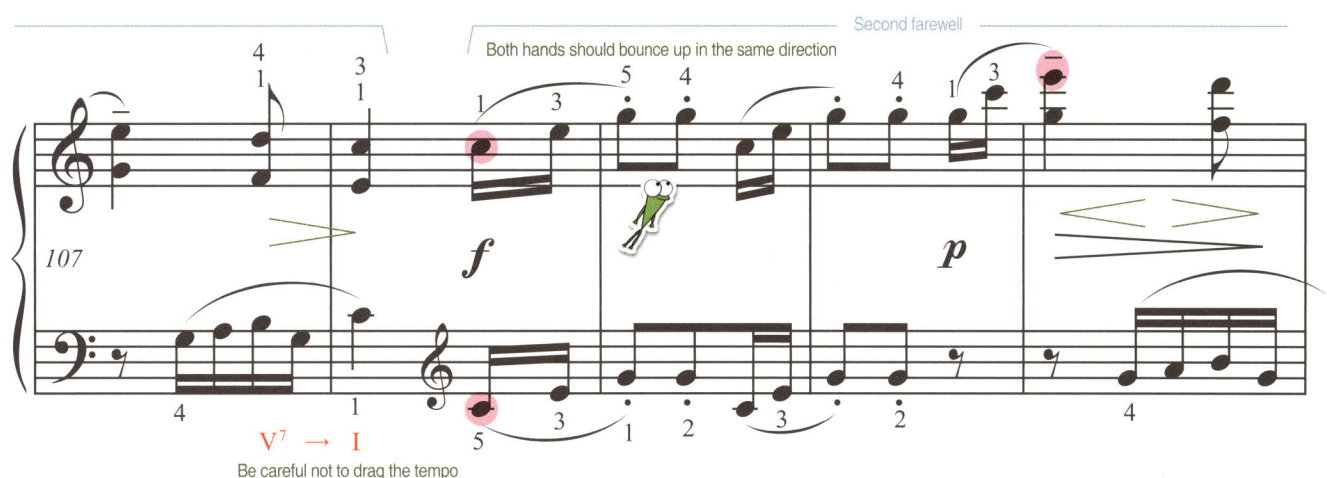

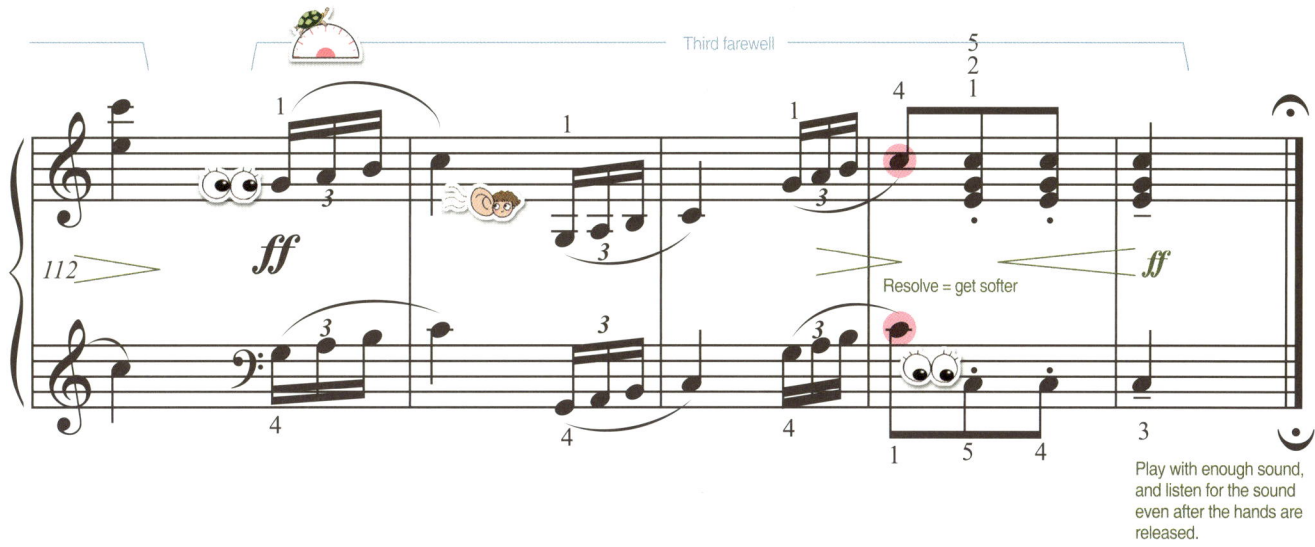

Sonatine Story

A tip to make stirring music: Before-sound and After-sound

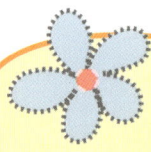 **Elise's Discovery: The Secret of Sound**

Once upon a time, the king of the Scale Kingdom returned to his palace after a long journey.
Countless citizens came crowding around the palace and cheered happily for his return.
The king's face was full of smile because he received a beautiful silver bell from the neighboring country.

"I hereby declare to my people that I will generously award whomever it is that can make
this silver bell sound the longest and the most beautiful."

Citizens rushed to stand in line to play the bell. The line was so long that it was endless.
One of those who stood in line was a sweet girl called Elise.
There were many people who played the bell, but nobody could really satisfy the king.
It was finally Elise's turn.

"Oh, how nervous I am! My heart is pounding.
But I'm sure I can make a beautiful sound if I use my arm and my wrist well.
I'll try to listen for the lingering sound and connect each sound well."

Elise stood in front of the bell with courage. She held the stick firmly and struck the bell while keeping
her wrist and her arm flexible. The beautiful sound of Elise's gong filled the entire palace.
Elise listened for how the sound of the bell faded and struck the bell again softly.

Elise struck the bell again and again, and the bell produced the most beautiful sound imaginable.
The king was very happy, and gave Elise a big prize.

Sonatine Story

❀ The three secrets of the Before-sound & After-sound revealed here!

1. Concentrate on fading, lingering sound.
   You want to know the secret Elise discovered?
   The piano's most important characteristic is that the sound always fades gradually after you strike the key.
   Don't forget to play a note, listen for how the sound fades, and then play the next note according
   to the lingering sound!

   M. Clementi Op. 36 No. 3, Movt. I

   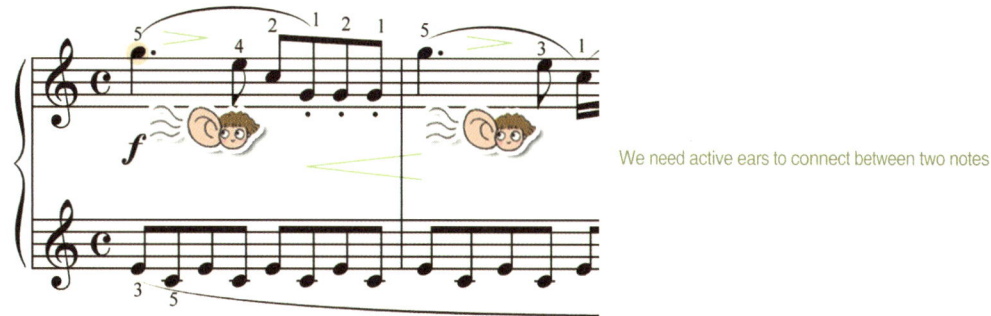

   We need active ears to connect between two notes

2. Quickly anticipate and imagine the upcoming dynamic level.

   Kuhlau Op. 55 No. 2, Movt. I

   We need to listen ahead when we are repeating a melody or as the music changes in the second theme.

3. When you stop, you can hear better!
   When you need 👂, STOP MOVING, OPEN YOUR EARS, AND IMAGINE THE UPCOMING SOUND!
   Remember, these three steps must happen quickly, almost at the speed of lightening!

   Kuhlau Op. 55 No. 2, Movt. I

M. Clementi Sonatine

Op. 36 No. 2 in G Major, 1st Movement

Ms. Silverplate's Smart Tips

🌼 **How can I make the most charming two-note slurs in the world?**

🌀 First, let's rotate the wrist in the shape of a snail's shell so that you can relax your wrist.
   Think of it as a warm-up before you can handle the second note of the slur splendidly.

🌀 Now, the fun begins...Before playing the first note, lower your wrist.

🌀 Then, rotate your wrist upward and let the second note of the slur bounce.

🌼 **The scale that begins with the pinky is always clumsy.**

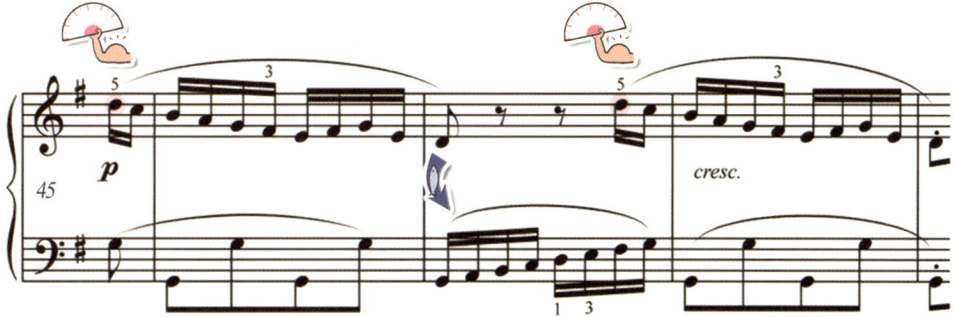

🌀 Bend your pinky so that you can see the end joint, and place the pinky on the key so that it's parallel to the keyboard.

🌀 The shape is right if you see the muscles of the pinky (on the palm side) bulging out.
   Lower the wrist slightly and prepare to pull on the key.

🌀 As soon as you play, bounce the wrist upward, and you will get a solid sound.

🌀 Play the rest of the notes in the scale as if you're pulling them away with your knuckles. Make sure your wrist is relaxed as you do this!

M. Clementi Op. 36 No. 2, 1st movt.

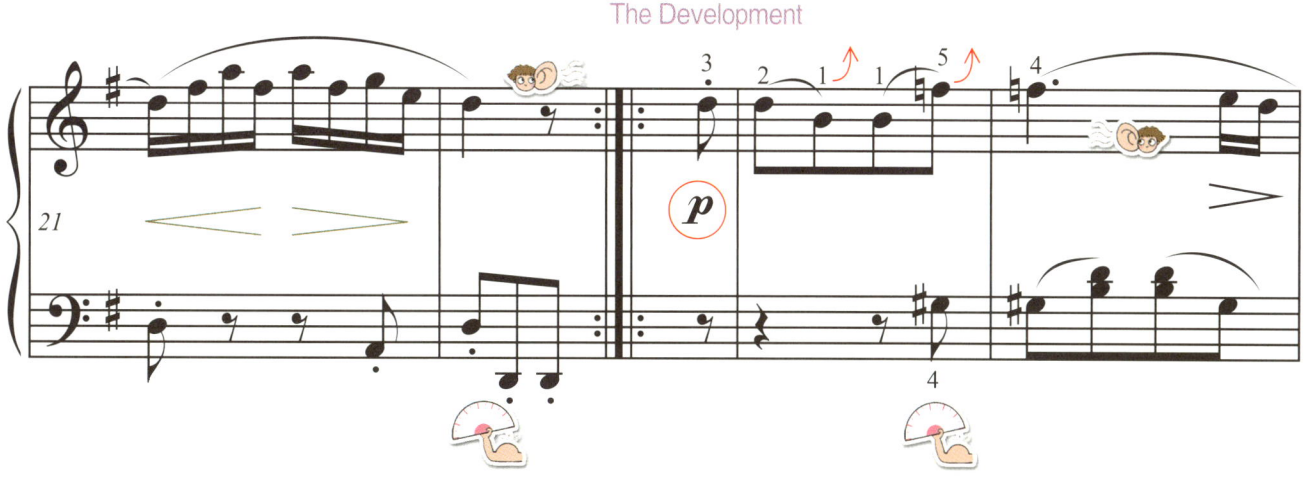
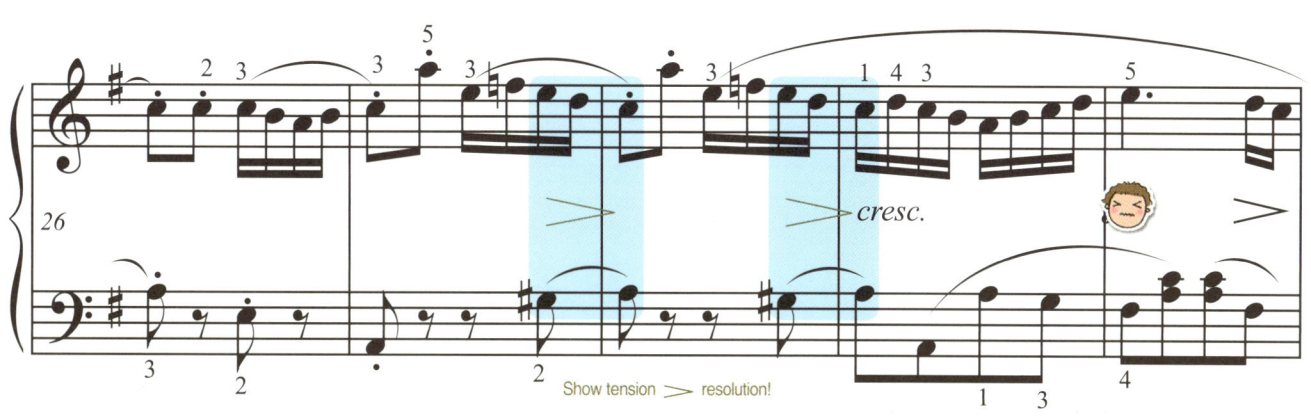
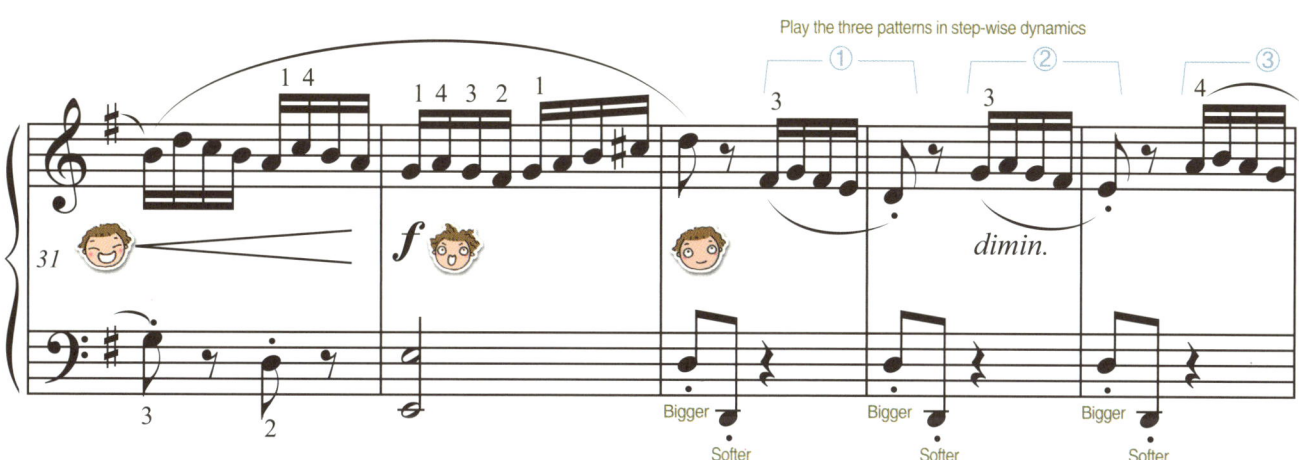
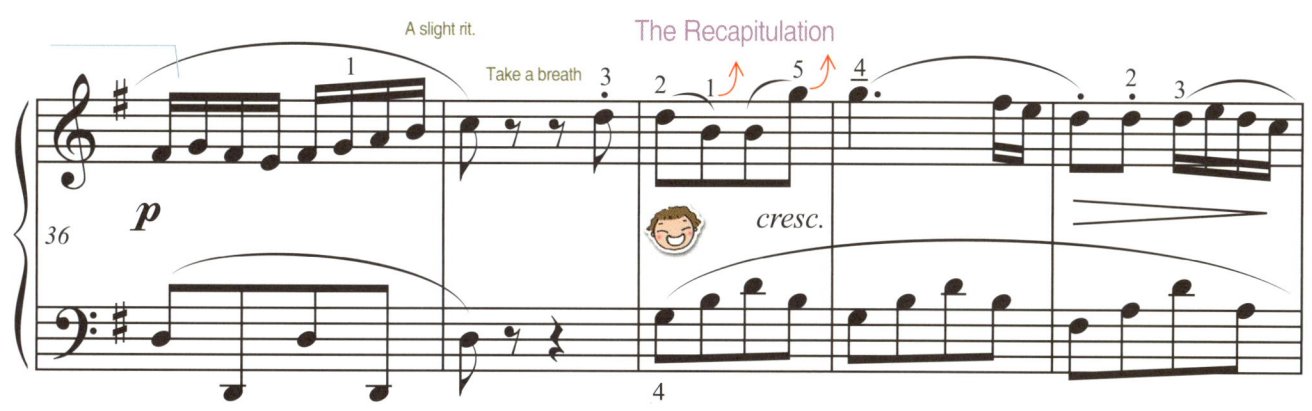

The ascending G-Major scale

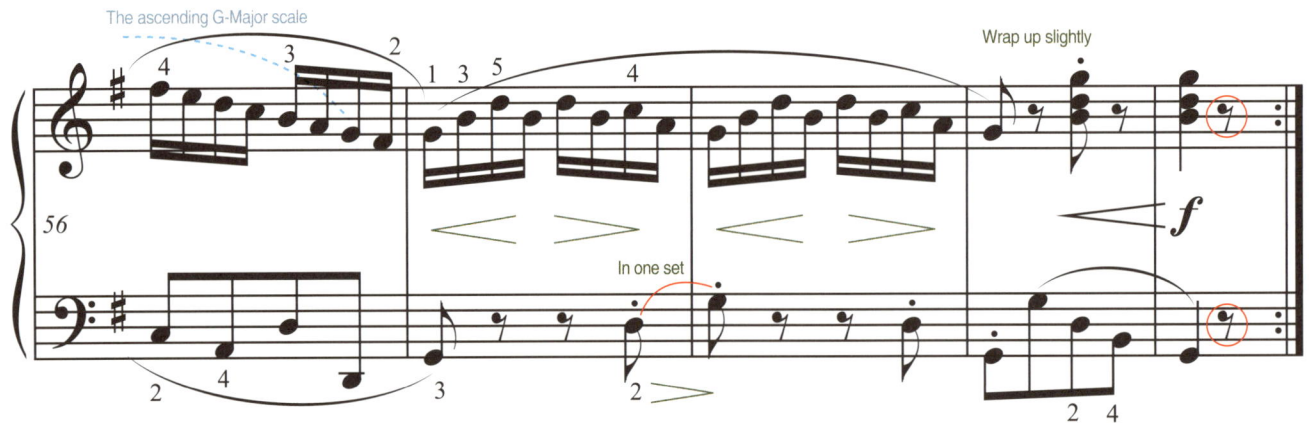

How can I show $<f$?

The first G in m. 59 is the end of a phrase, so play softly. But do the $<f$ immediately afterward, as if to overwhelm p. End majestically.

It's hard at first, but try practicing it 3 times. It'll get better!

Memo

Sonatine **Story**

Treasure Hunt! ...No, wait...it's a Scale Hunt!
3, 2, 1 → Go!

In 1750, a pirate ship was crossing the Atlantic ocean.
The pirates were excited at the thought of all the treasures they would soon discover.
They finally landed on the Scale Island and opened up their treasure map. Here it is!

1. Location of the scale treasure
   Look at the key signature and the accidentals and guess which key this scale is in.
   - When accidentals appear, you know that the scale is in a different key from the key of the piece.
   - But if there are no accidentals, the scale will be in the same key as the piece.
   - The C Major scale doesn't necessarily start with the note C! Don't let the first note of the scale throw you off! (In fact, scales will usually begin on a different note!)

2. Possible traps
   Beware the chromatic half-tones!

3. Warning - You must find all these scales in **3** minutes!

 OK, the hunt begins now...

1. Which scale is the one marked in blue?

M. Clementi Op. 36 No. 1, Movt. I

2. Which scale is the one marked in blue?

M. Clementi Op. 36 No. 2, Movt. III

3. Which scale is the one marked in blue?

M. Clementi Op. 36 No. 4, Movt. I

4. Which scale is the one marked in blue?

Kuhlau Op. 55 No. 2, Movt. II

✦ Now that you've found the treasure, you must use them well!

1. Do a slight crescendo toward the leading-tone,
   and get slightly softer on the 1st scale degree.

✦ Don't forget those enticing chromatic tones.

- They sneak in sometimes, or sometimes scales are fully chromatic.

1. Notice that the distance between tones has narrowed, and play them as if the keyboard is sticky
   (as you play the next note, be sluggish in releasing the previous note - slightly overlap the notes).
2. We must be able to hear that these chromatic tones are strange and exotic, right?
3. If you do a slight crescendo as you go up and a slight decrescendo as you come down,
   the entire piece will become livelier.

M. Clementi Sonatine

Op. 36 No. 2 in G Major, 3rd Movement

Ms. Silverplate's Smart Tips

🌼 **How can I not make things boring when things repeat?**

You don't have to articulate every note in the same volume.
For example, in the 3/8 time signature, think of each measure as one. This way, phrases become more natural.

🌀 First, play only the first notes of each measure and imagine the other notes in your head.
   (Here, think of four measures as one breath)

🌀 In these four measures, do a crescendo and a diminuendo.

🌼 **Trill and octave accompaniments scare me!**

🌀 Why not try to write out each note of the trill?
   Remember, trills start from above in pieces in the classical period.

🌀 If you're slowing down with trills, practice as the following:
   You're essentially aligning the left hand bass notes with the right hand.

🌀 Last but not least, start the trill softly and then do a crescendo until the end.
   (as if coke is bubbling!)

🌀 Let's now look at the left-hand accompaniment. If your hand is too small...
   Play the lower A short (staccato) and play the top A softer as an echo.

M.Clementi Op. 36 No. 2, 3rd movt.

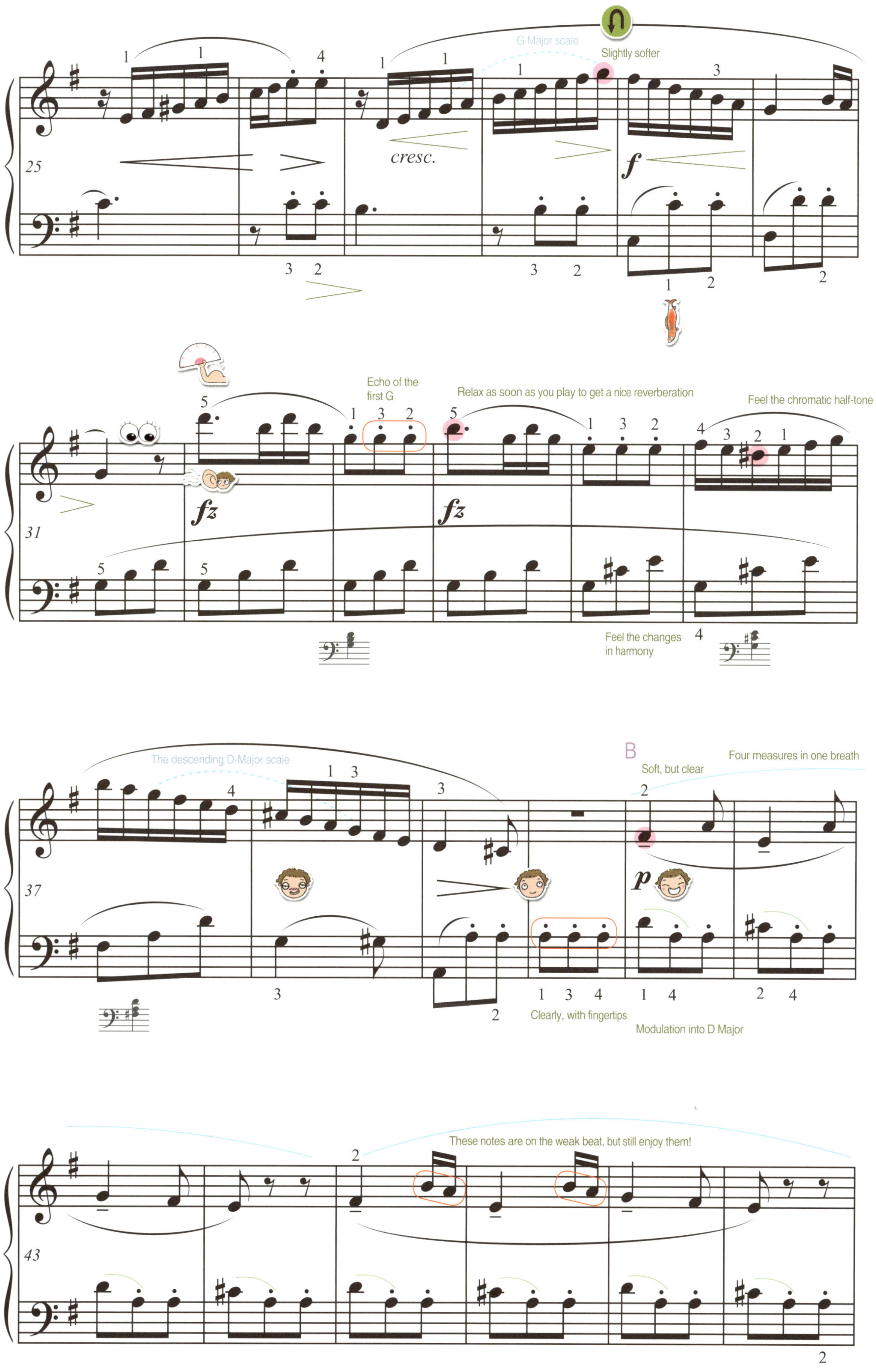
G Major scale
Slightly softer
cresc.
Echo of the first G
Relax as soon as you play to get a nice reverberation
Feel the chromatic half-tone
Feel the changes in harmony
The descending D-Major scale
B
Soft, but clear
Four measures in one breath
Clearly, with fingertips
Modulation into D Major
These notes are on the weak beat, but still enjoy them!

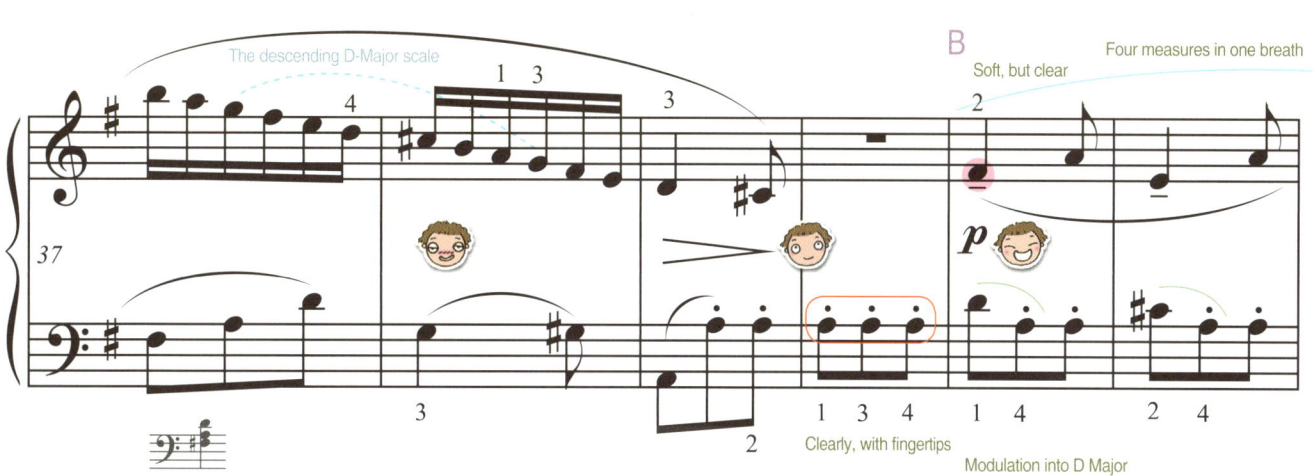

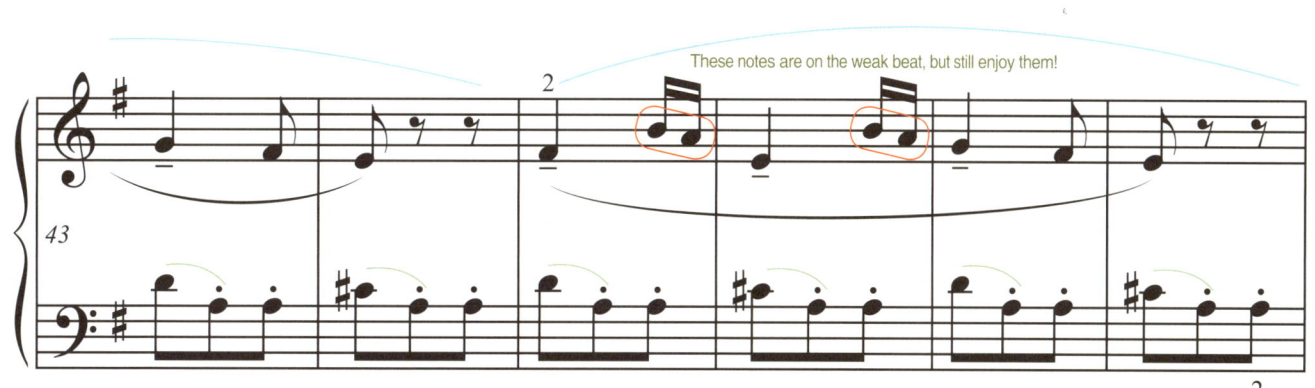

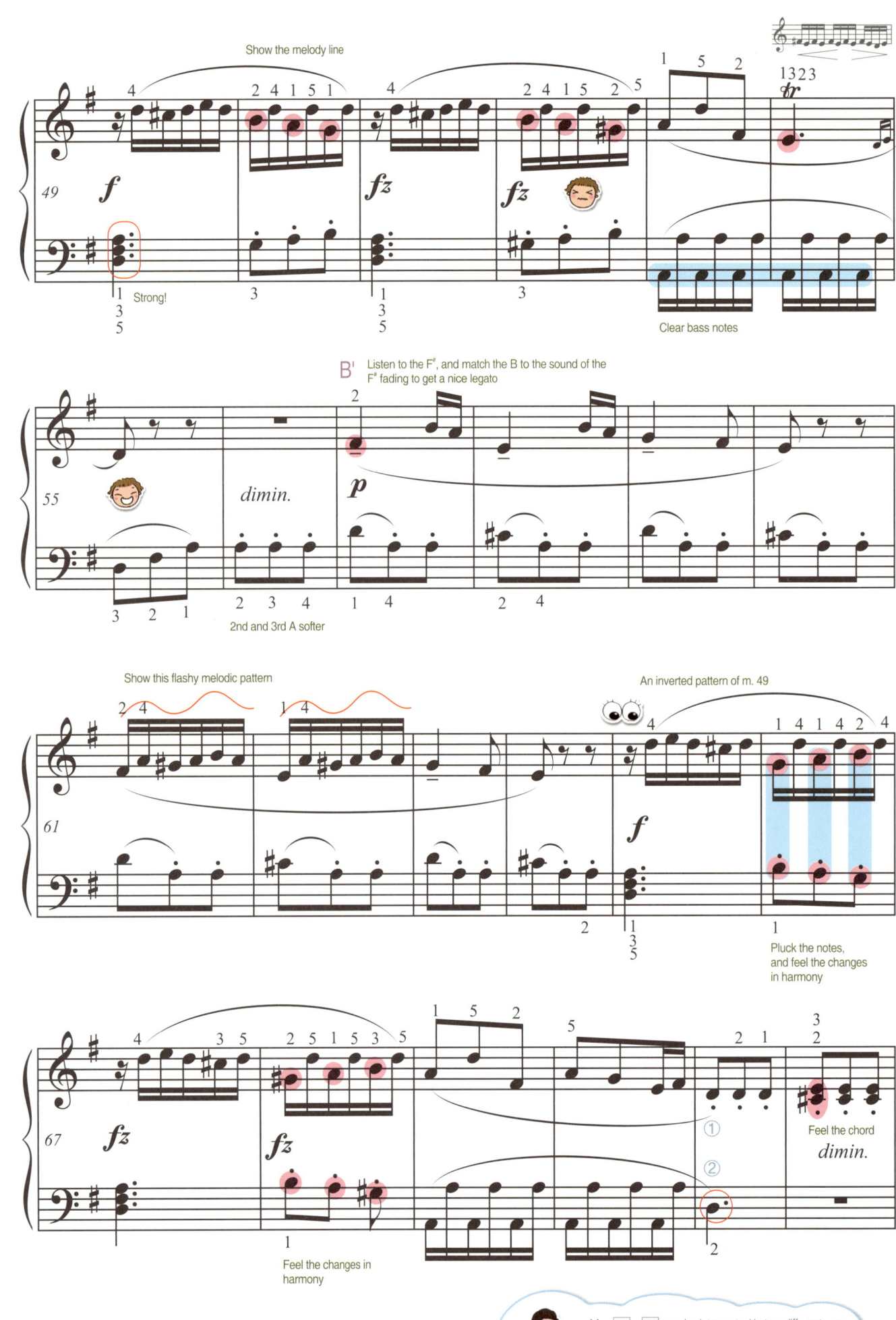

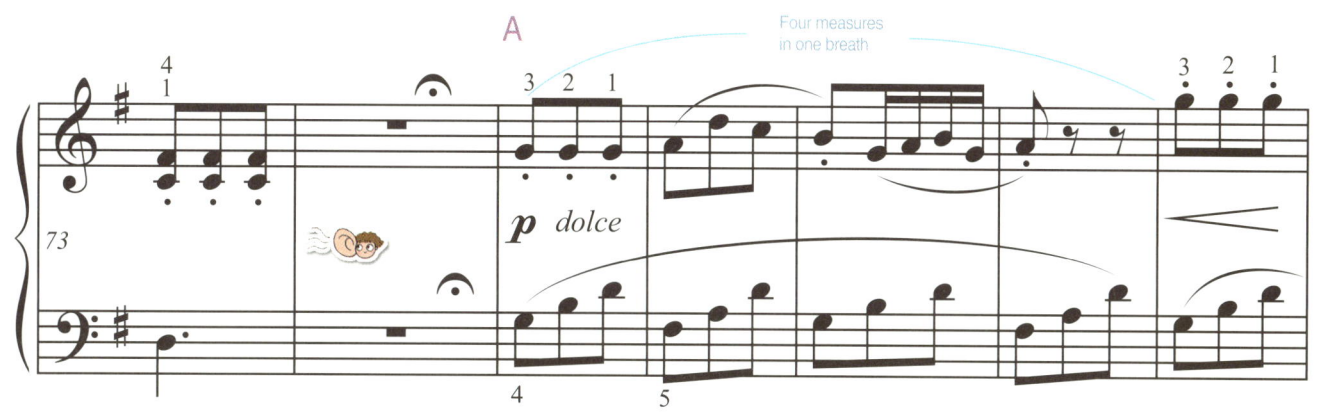
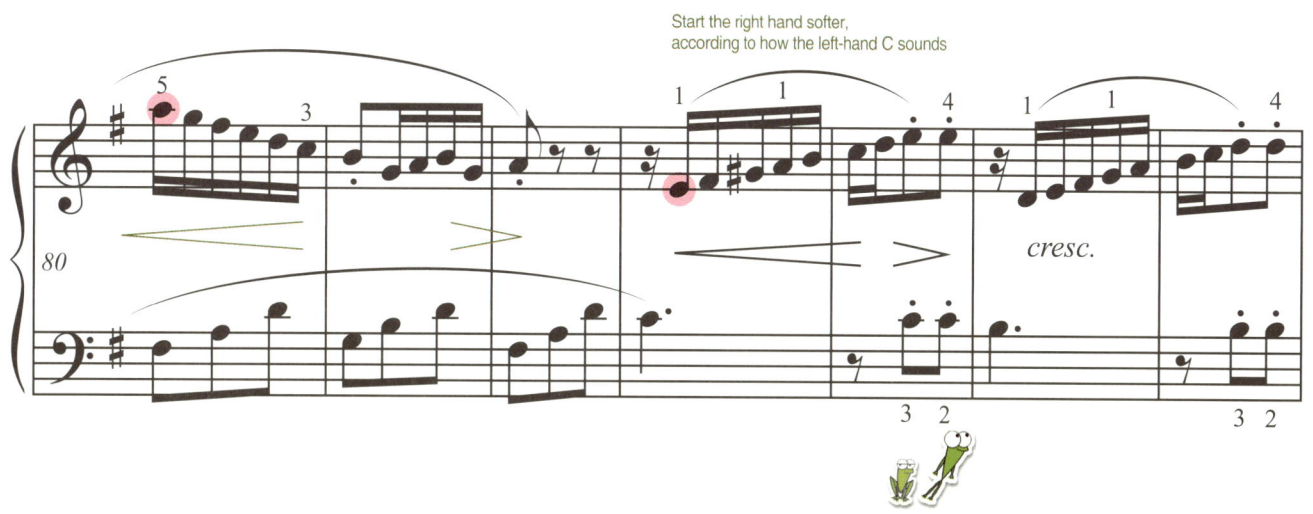

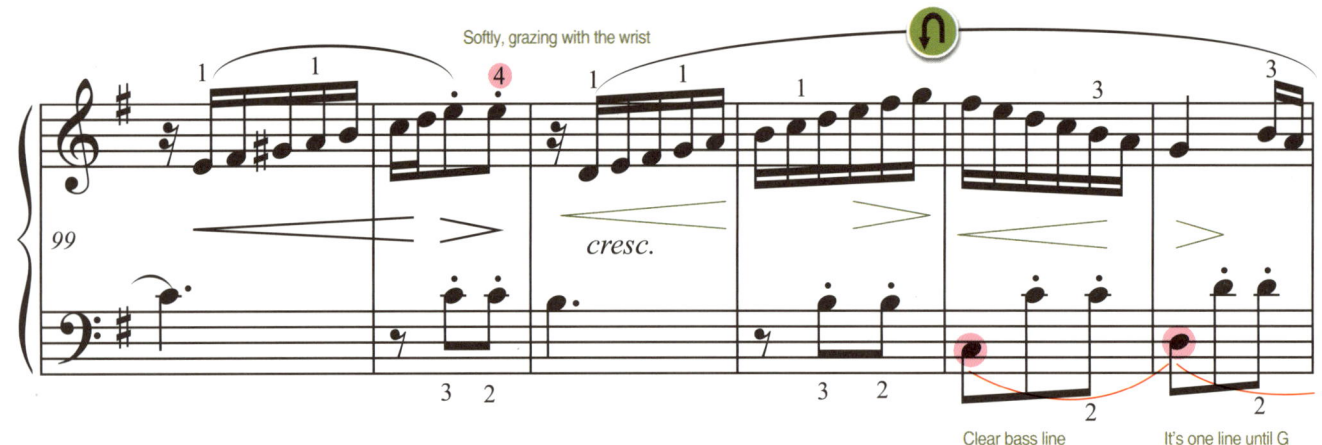

The Coda

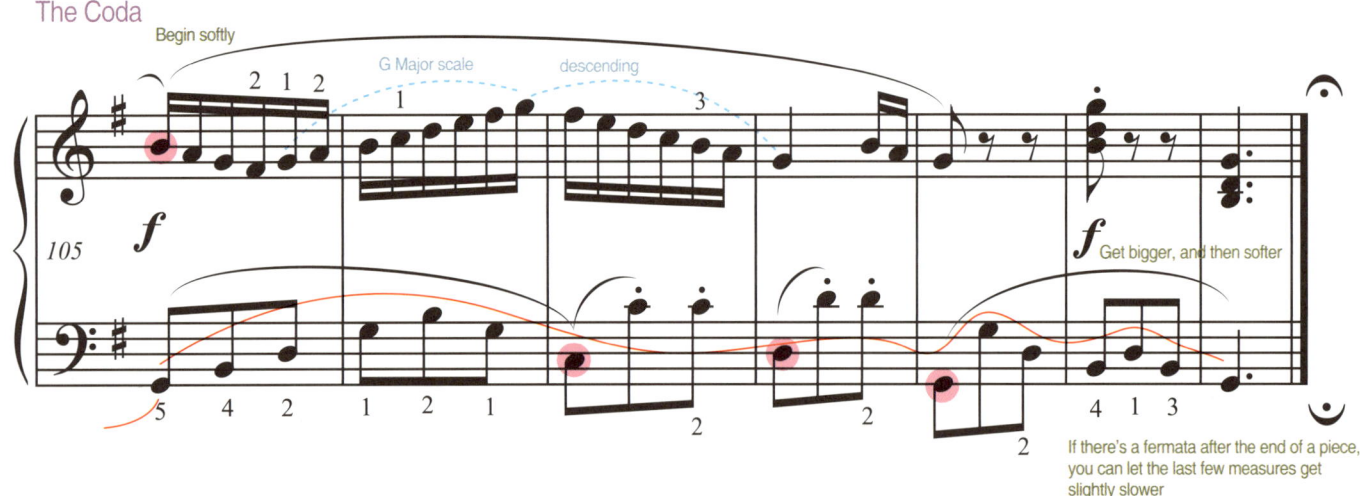

Memo

If you "preview," you'll make fewer mistakes...

Sonatine **Story**

Let's visit the blog of Ms. **Preview**!

Ms. Preview has the biggest eyes in the Icon village, and everybody loves her! She's even appeared on TV for saving a girl called Pearl in a subway station; Pearl fell onto the track and Preview fished her out.

❀ Here's what the legendary pedagogue, Ms. Silverplate has left on Ms. **Preview**'s visitor page:

> I am happy to introduce my best pupil Ms. **Preview**.
> As I have explained in *Secrets to Scales*, seemingly unimportant things like when and where pianists focus their eyes can make a huge difference in piano playing.
> For example, I had a student who couldn't play the leaps well, so I told him to look ahead with his eyes to where he will play next.
> With this advice, this student was able to overcome his difficulty.
> He no longer kept stopping musical flow by not looking ahead.
> If you can befriend Ms. **Preview** icon, you will be able to play any leaps with ease.
> Also, remember that your sight-reading skills will improve if you can master leaps.

❀ Diary - **My secret** to better leaps: head → eyes → hands

From my experiences, I can say that mastering leaps comes in three steps.
- 1st step : imagining the second note of the leap in my mind
- 2nd step : quickly turning my eyes on the score to the next measure
    Preparation is the key! With quick leaps, I must be able to respond quickly to what is to come.
- 3rd step : moving my hand quickly to whatever that follows

I hope I can share my secrets with my friends who also play the piano.

M. Clementi Op. 36 No. 1, Movt. III

On the pinky, angle of your wrist and your forearm must be correct

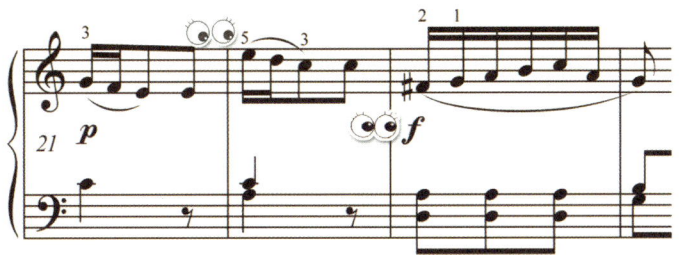

✿ Photos - My best friend, Before-sound

I am very close to Before-sound because I have to work very closely with him in changing the atmosphere of music in big leaps.

Dear friends, be sure to think of dynamic changes after leaping. Look at the example below.

M. Clementi Op. 36 No. 2, Movt. III

M. Clementi Sonatine

Op. 36 No. 3 in C Major, 3rd Movement

Ms. Silverplate's Smart Tips

🌼 **What is the U-Turn?**

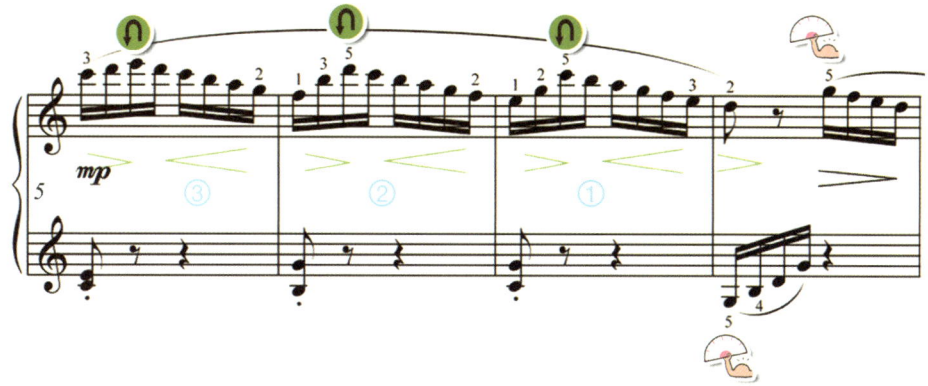

🍀 U-Turn icon means that you should do a diminuendo as you reach the highest note.

🍀 Lift your wrist slightly so that the top note doesn't stick out.

🍀 Doing a crescendo as the melody line descends can also be thrilling!

🌼 **My fingers get tangled up in continuous arpeggios.**

🍀 Group four notes into one and bounce on the first note!
As you bounce (like on a trampoline), make sure your wrist goes up at the same time.
Let your wrist slightly bend toward your pinky.

🍀 After bouncing on the first note, let the rest of the notes follow in one sweep.
The trick is to play the second note softer than the first.

> **Level up!** There is a similar pattern in Schubert's Impromptu Op. 90 No. 4 in A-flat Major.
> It's difficult, but give it a try!

M. Clementi Op. 36 No. 3, 3rd movt.

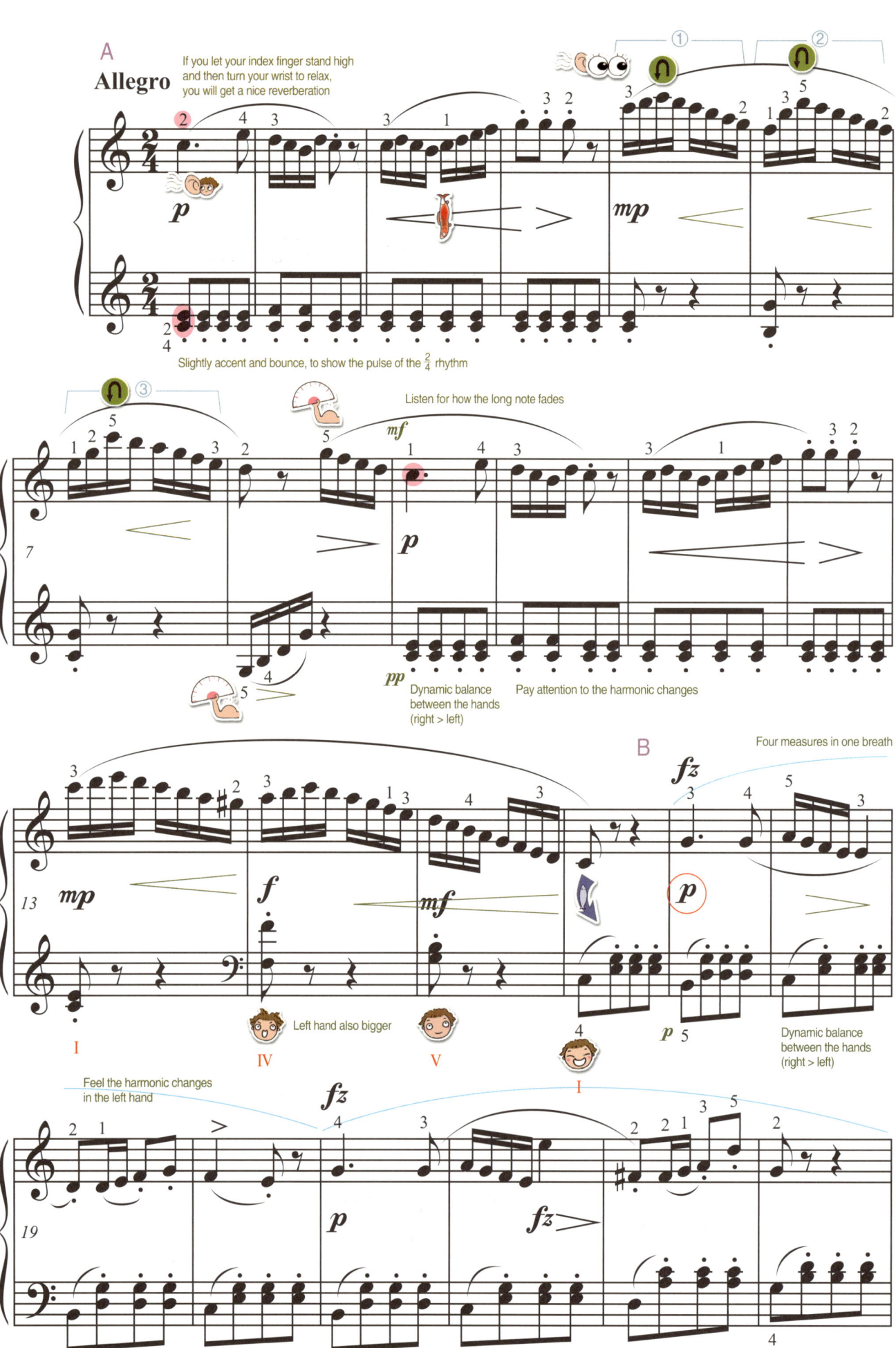

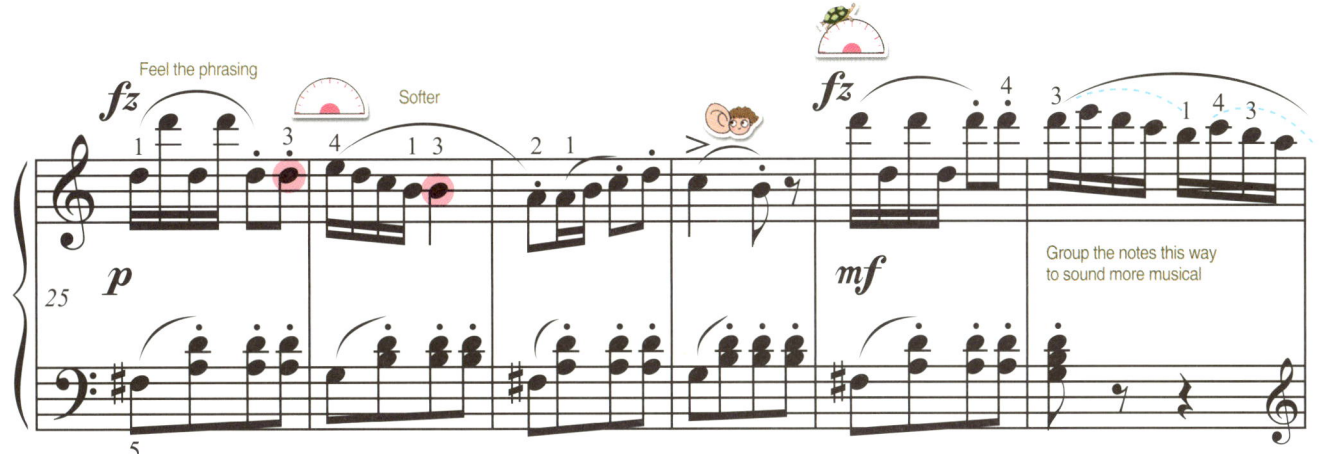
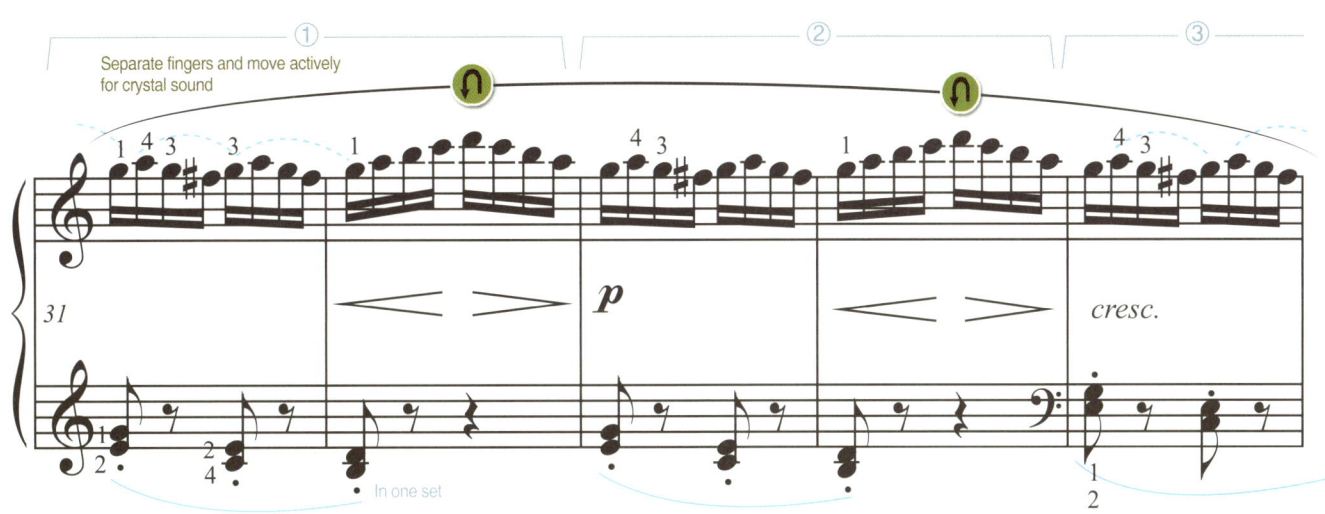
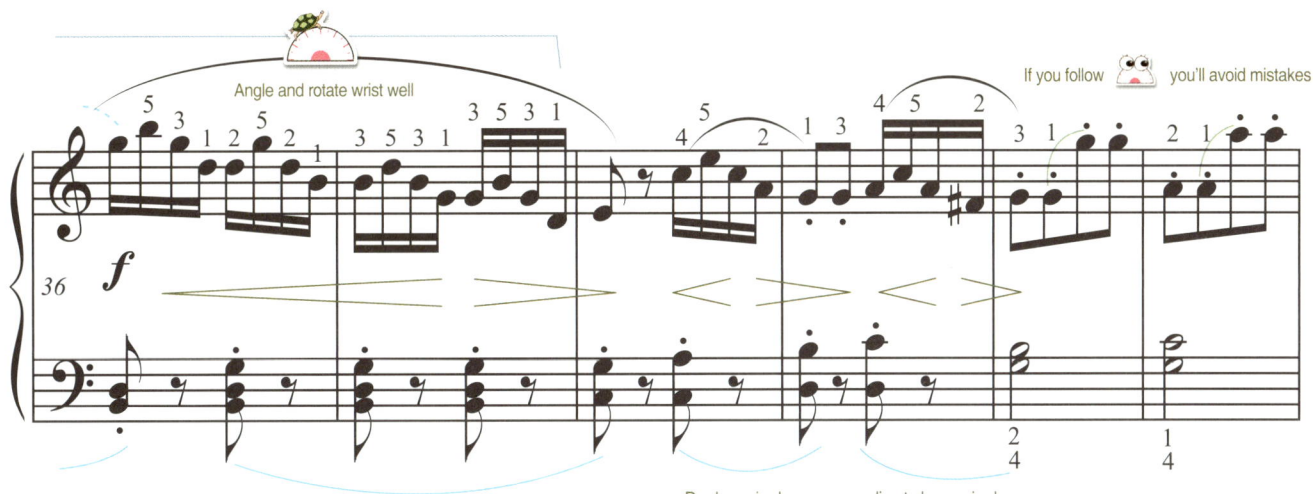
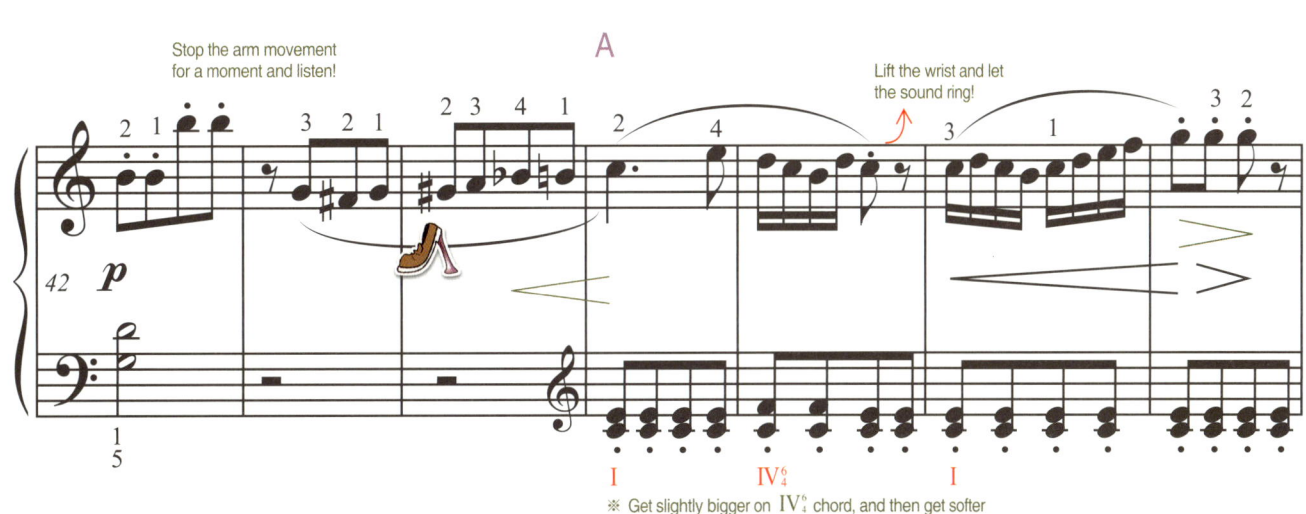

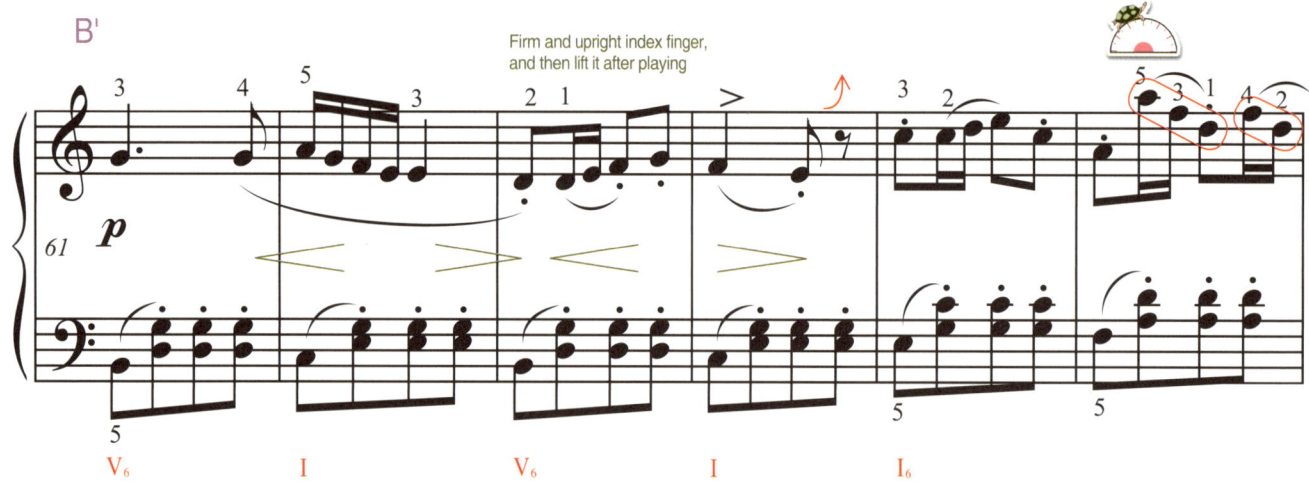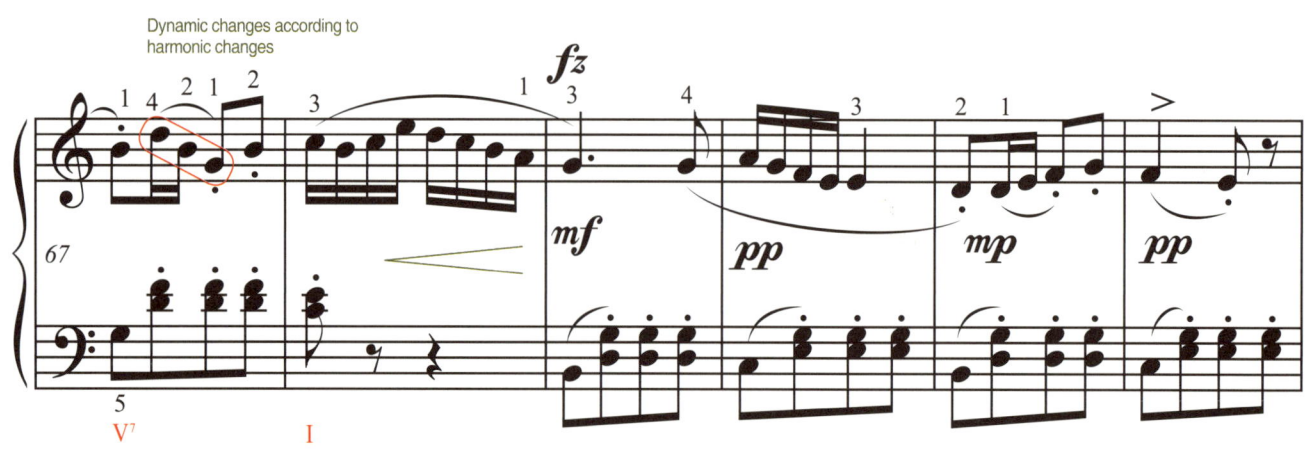

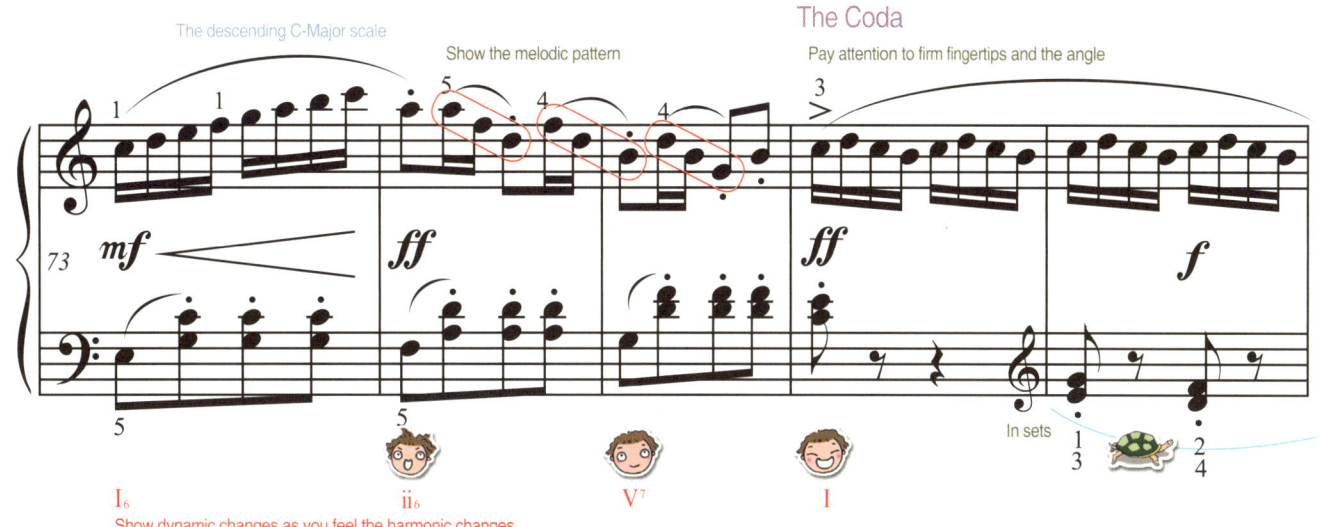

Sonatine Story

The scariest horror movie in the world...
"Breath Holding" is finally released in theaters!

 The hidden story of the "Three Little Pigs" - "The Breath of the Wolf"

It was a hot, sunny summer day. The wolf, who hadn't eaten anything in a month, was plodding along aimlessly. This was the same wolf that was once famous for capturing kids with wobbly hands in the SuperFastForward kingdom. It had been also famous for blowing away houses made of straws and sticks with his monstrous breath, but those days were long gone.
As it was walking around, the wolf heard a voice.
  "Oink oink, clunk clunk, let's build a house! Oink oink!"
The wolf smiled at once and hid behind a tree to observe the little piggy. But his hope turned into shock upon seeing the piggy's house...it was a three-story brick house, too strong to be blown away with the wolf's breath!
But the wolf gathered itself.
  "I won't surrender! I'm sure I can blow away this house too, using my solid technique. Let me start slowly... it's been a while since I've done this."

1. Open the mouth, breathe in and expand the stomach
2. Then breathe out slowly, until my stomach is flat again

If I get used to it, I can breathe in and expand my stomach all at once. Yes...I can see my six packs are still there. I'm going to finish this in one try. WHOOOOO~~"
The wolf's heartbreaking last attempt, - will he succeed?

 Surprise mission!
Do abdominal breathing **three times** to move onto the next page.

Sonatine Story

Why do we need to hold the breath?

Is it difficult to make the beginning of a piece or a new theme stylish?
A new beginning always needs excitement!
The silence that follows a quick breathing-in sharpens the ear and prepares you for the music to come.
If you can breathe in and then hold your breath right before playing, you've already come halfway.

A trip to the Sonatine mountain range!

1. As you hold your breath, think of the tempo and be ready to listen!

2. For a better breath control, do abdominal breathing quickly for ten times.

3. If you can control your breathing in four-measure units, you can reach the top of the mountain in three hours!
   (But make sure your breathing isn't noticeable; when you breathe out, do it gradually to save your breath)

Remember :
Before the second theme or the recapitulation, you may begin to forget this technique, so remember the keyword "Hold the Breath!"

M. Clementi Op. 36 No. 1, Movt. III

M. Clementi Sonatine

Op. 36 No. 3 in C Major, 1st Movement

Ms. Silverplate's Smart Tips

🌼 **What should I do with a really really long crescendo?**

Try doing smaller dynamic changes according to harmonic progression.

- First, make sure your sound is firm and clear!
  It's more important to make every chord sound solid than the crescendo itself.
  Bounce on each chord as if bouncing on a trampoline.

- Chords can be distinguished as either consonant or dissonant.
  If you emphasize dissonant chords and make the consonant chords sound softer
  as if they're resolving the dissonant chords, your playing will be full of life!
  Think of each dissonance > consonance chords as one set as you play.

- But if every dissonant chord is equally loud, it will surely sound crude.
  To prevent this from happening, let each dissonant chord get bigger,
  in a stepwise dynamic development, and then do a diminuendo afterwards.

The ultimate challenge! If you practice ahead of time, it will be easier. Trust me!

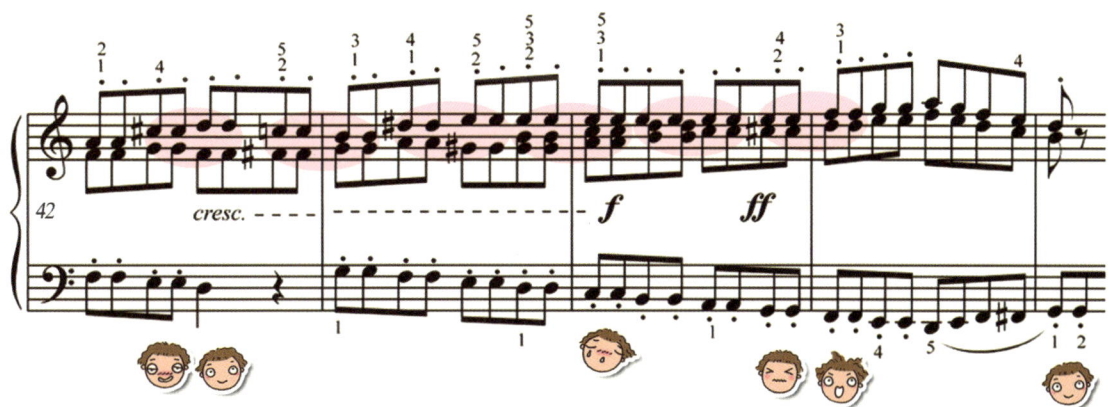

M. Clementi Op. 36 No. 3, 1st movt.

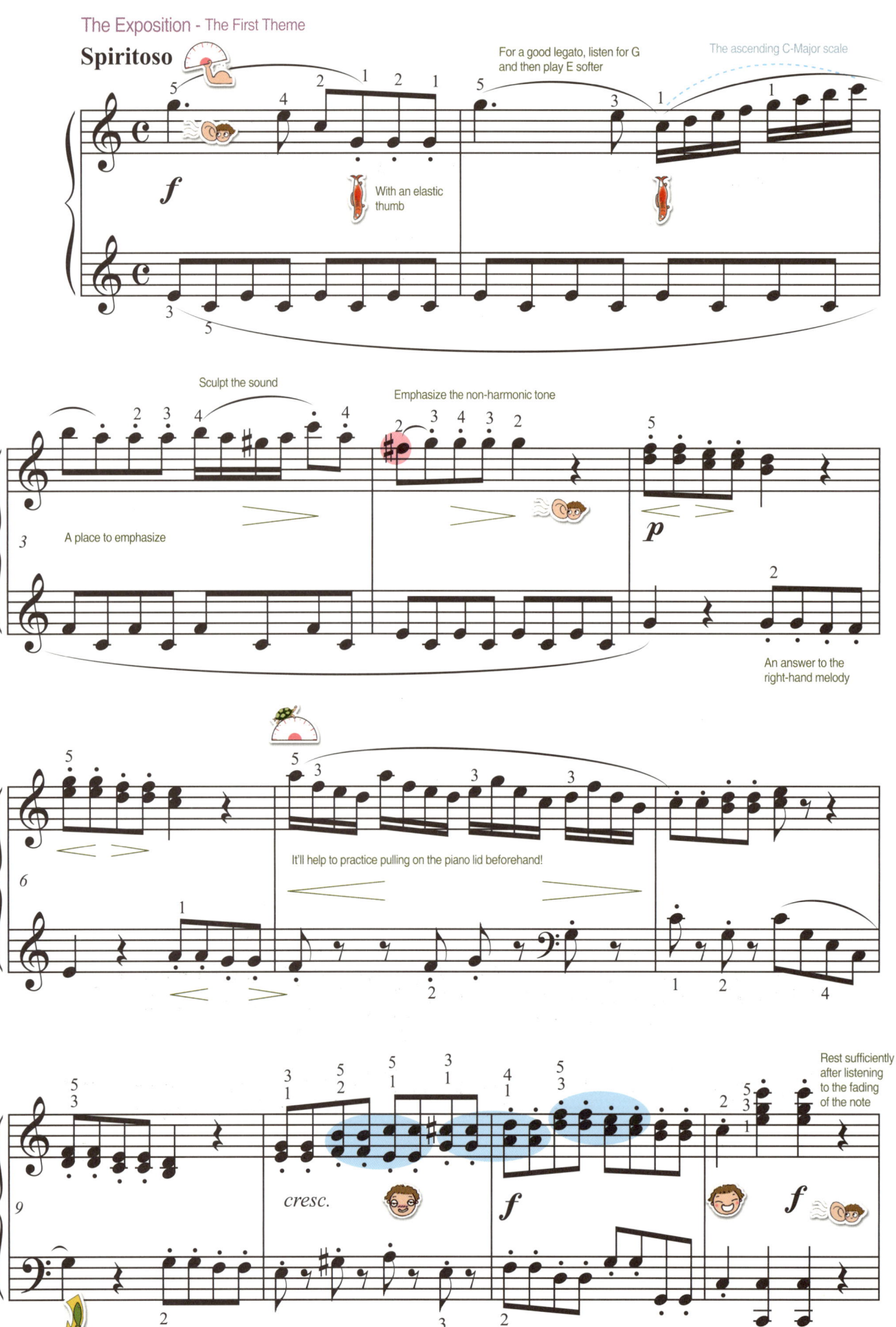

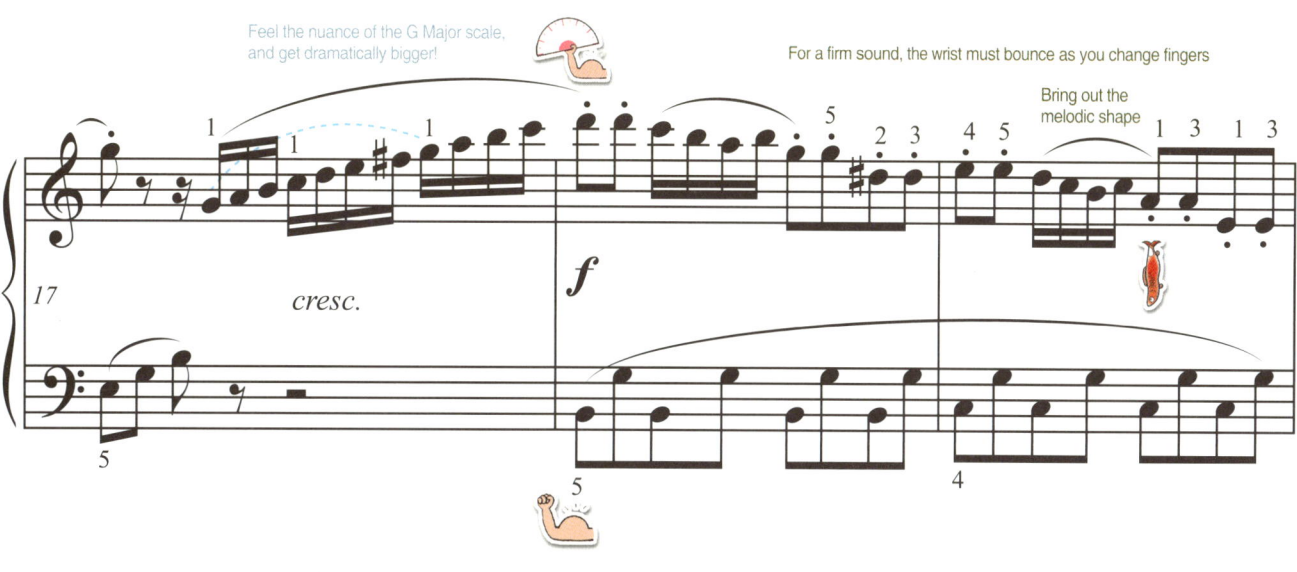
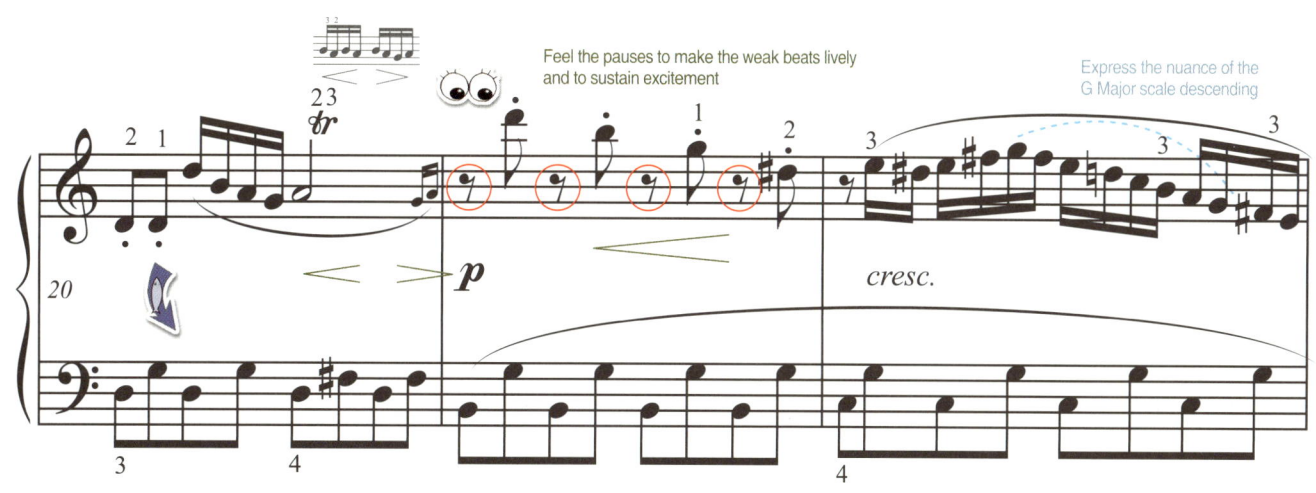

Don't forget to let the left hand participate in the action of the right hand!

The Development
Feel the suspense in the pause!
Feel the movement of the bones in the wrist joint
legato

Express the nuance of the C Major scale ascending
Carry the weight of the arm in the fingertips and pluck the keys
Imagine *ff*!
A climax!
Let the left hand help

It's slightly sadder all of a sudden
Play the harmonic "columns" first and feel the progression

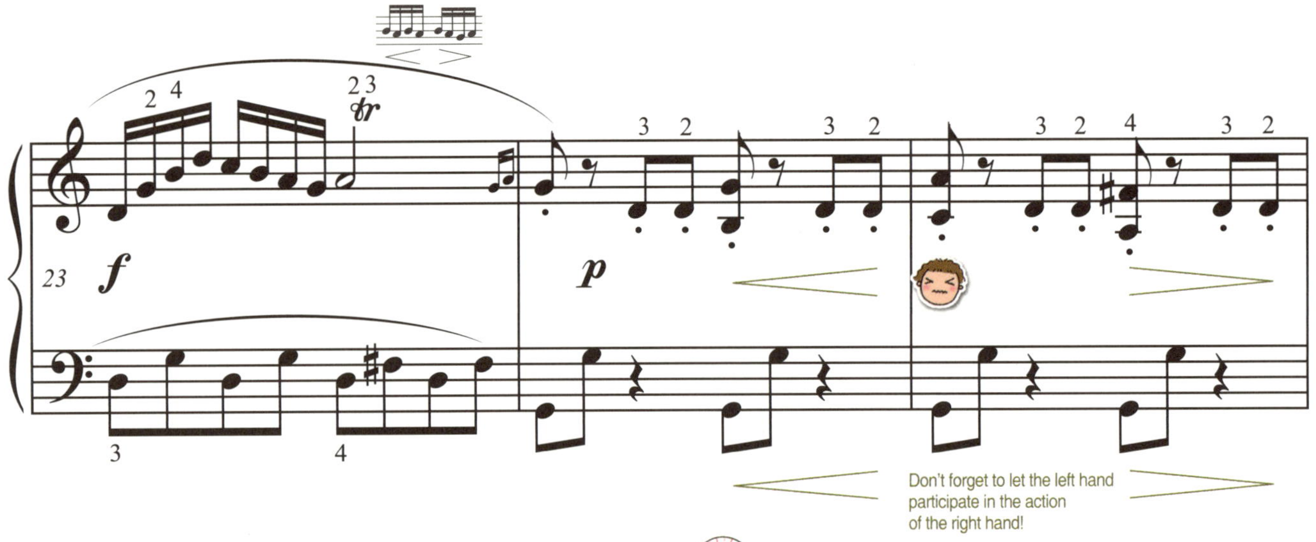

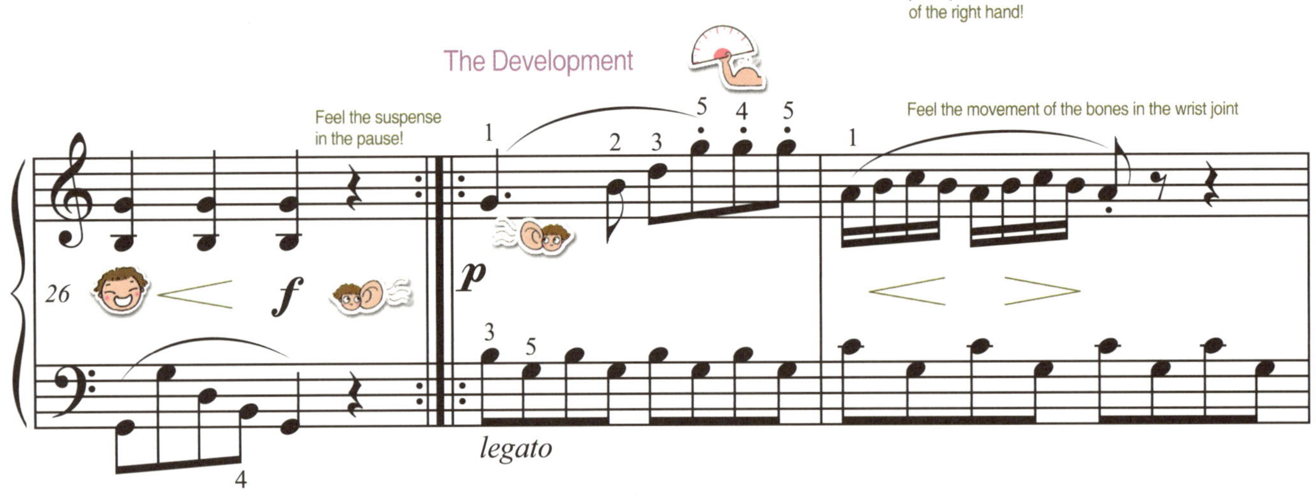

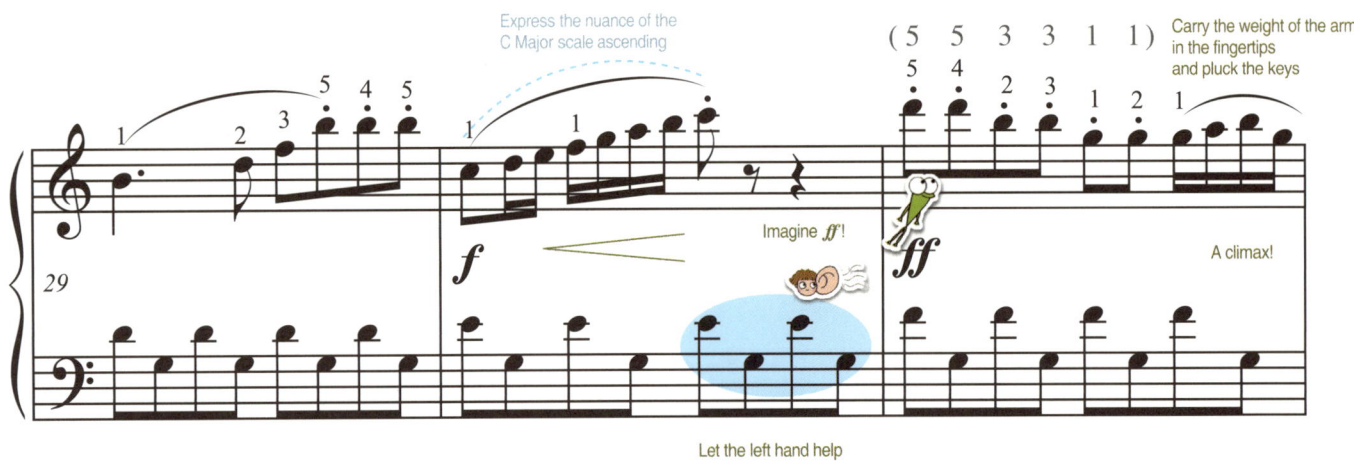

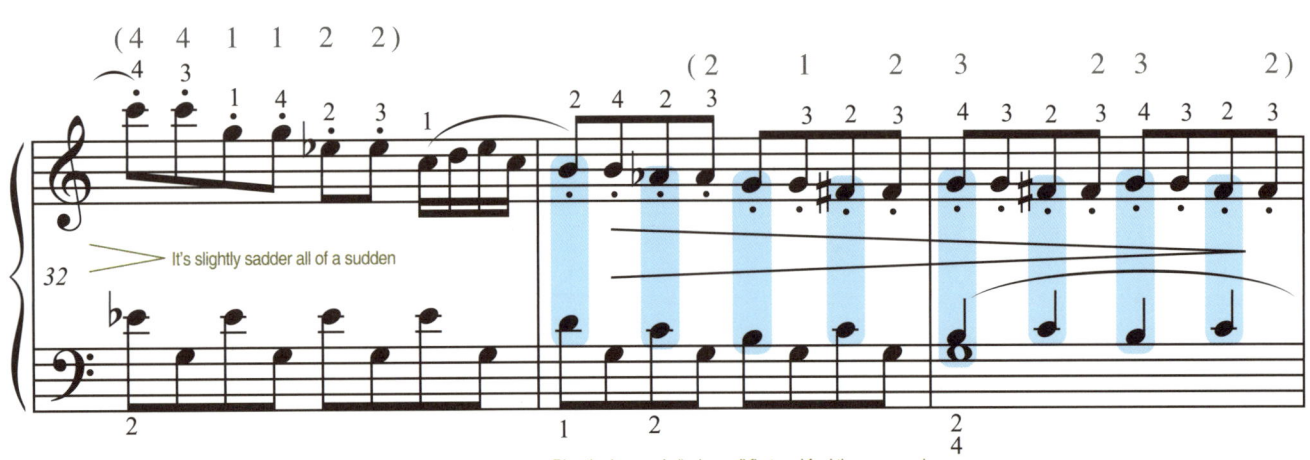

The Recapitulation - The First Theme

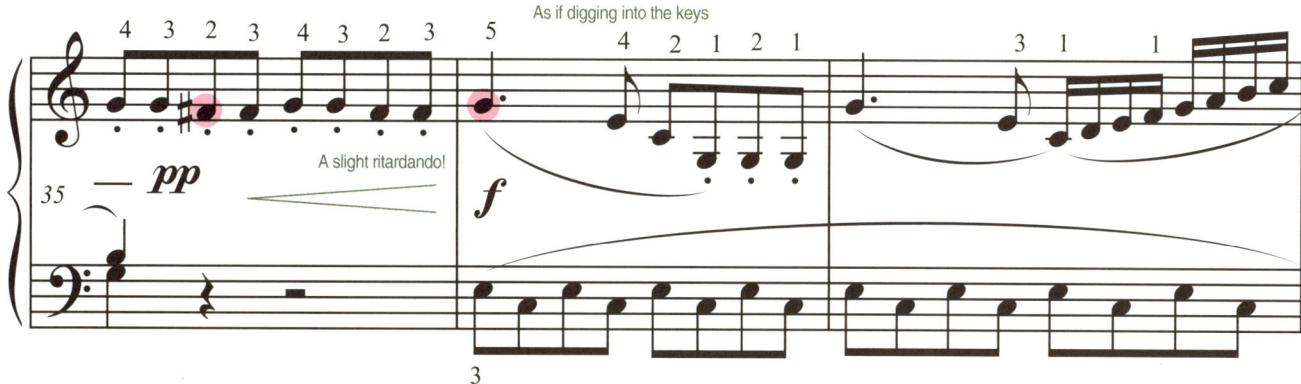
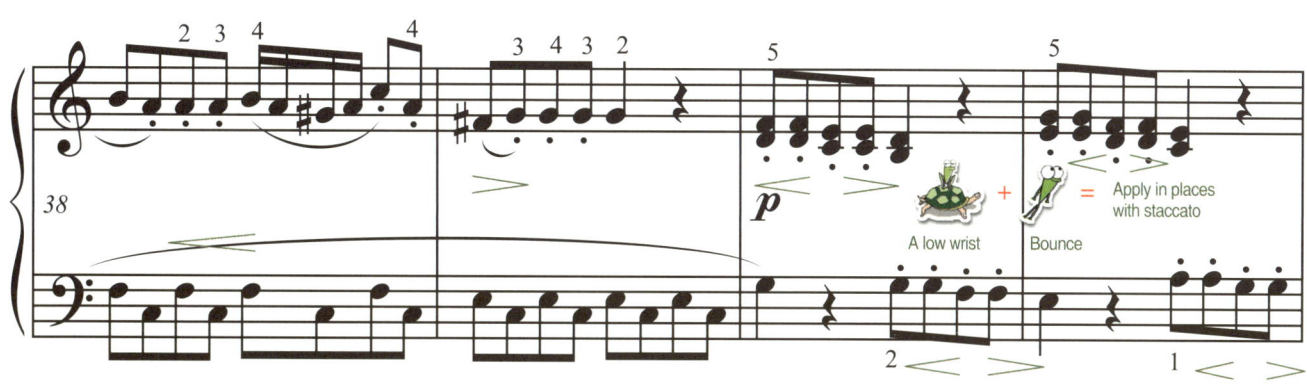
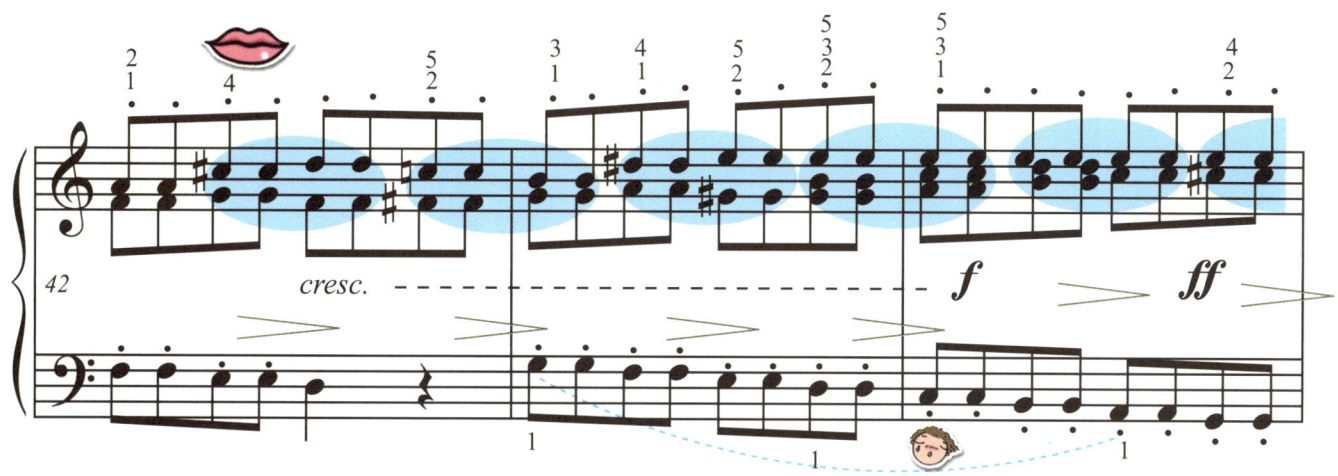
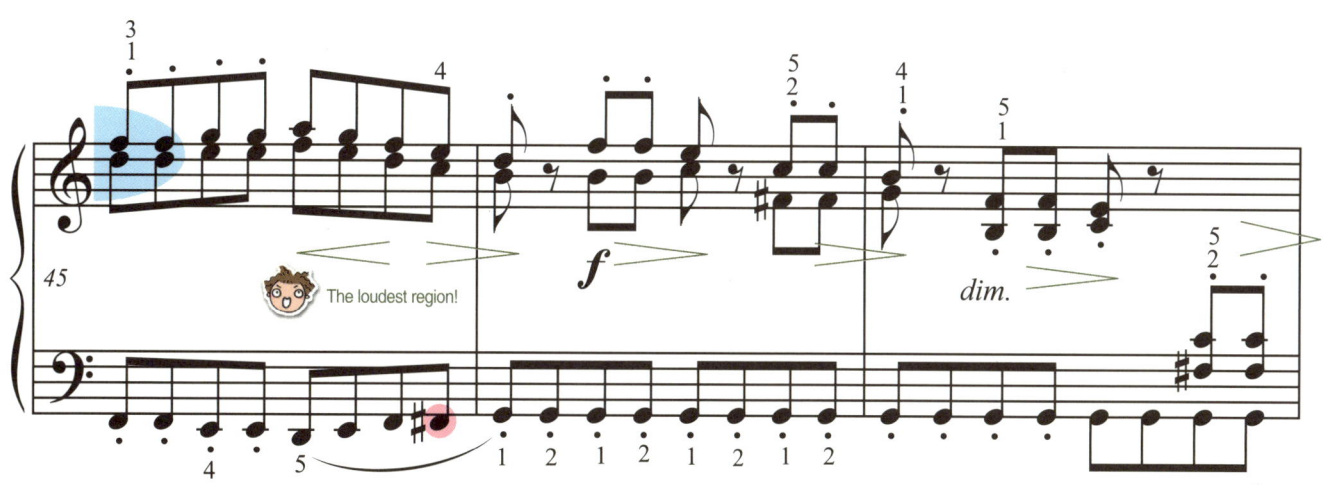

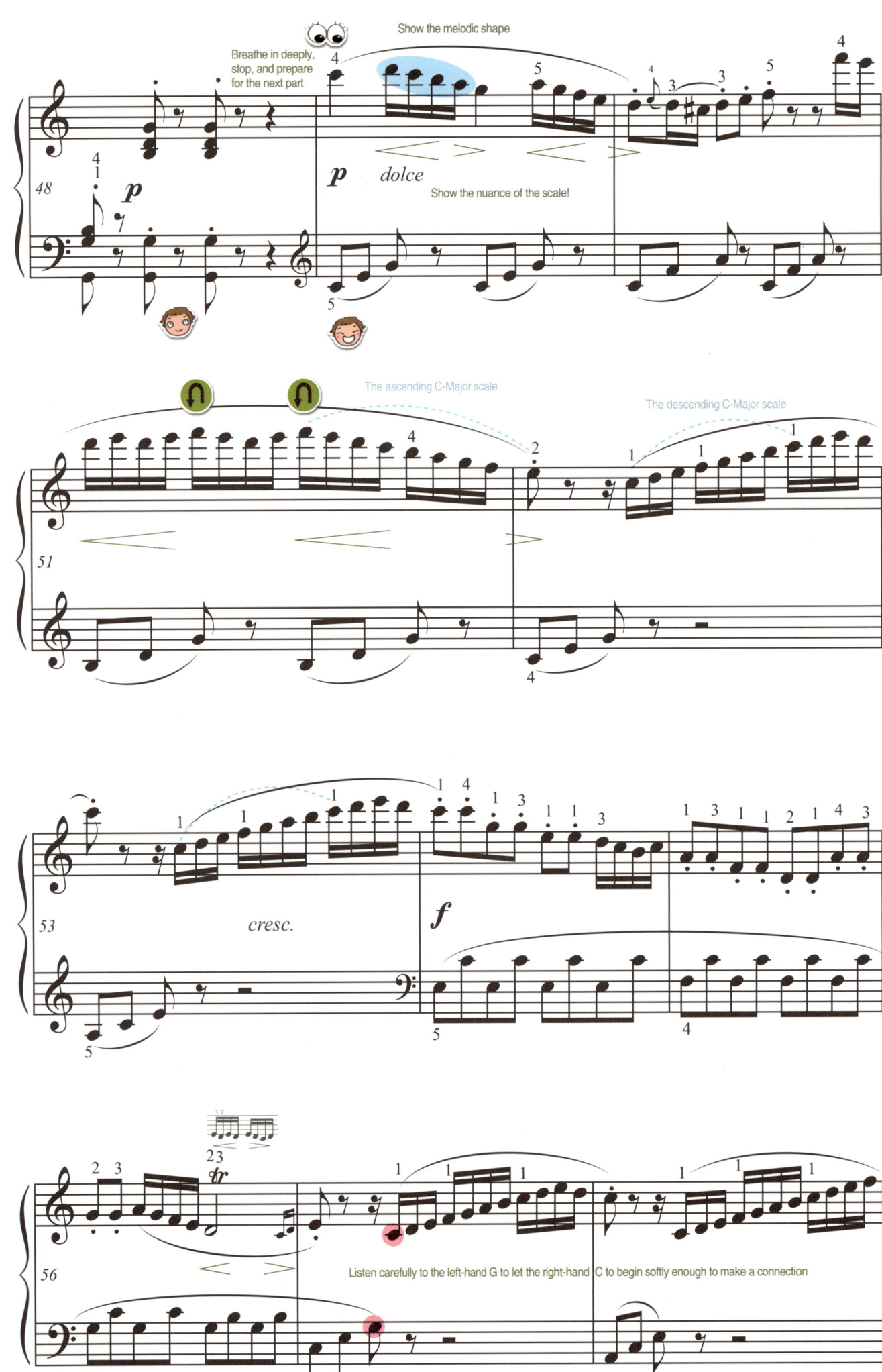

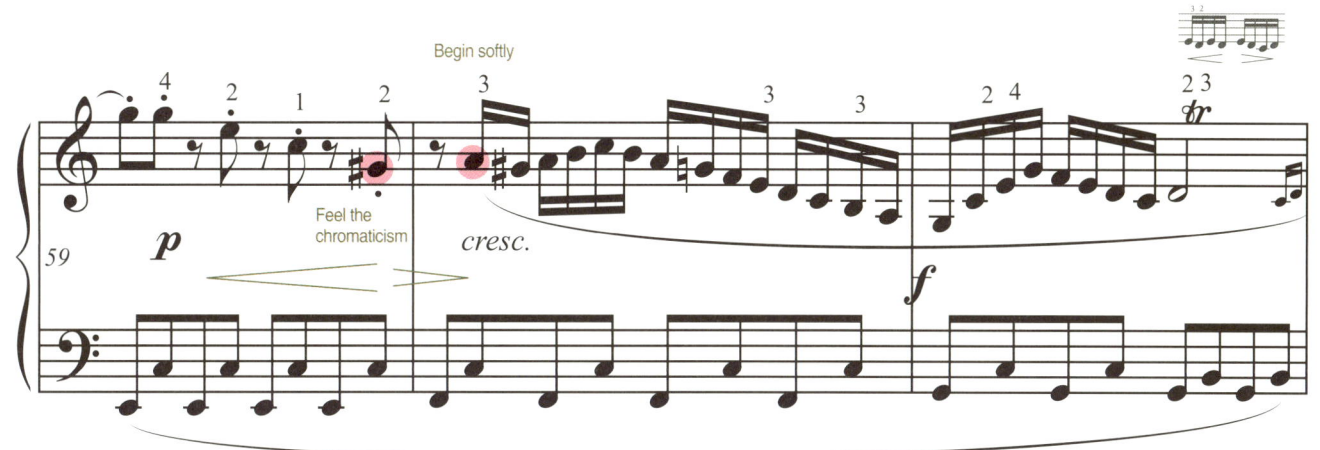
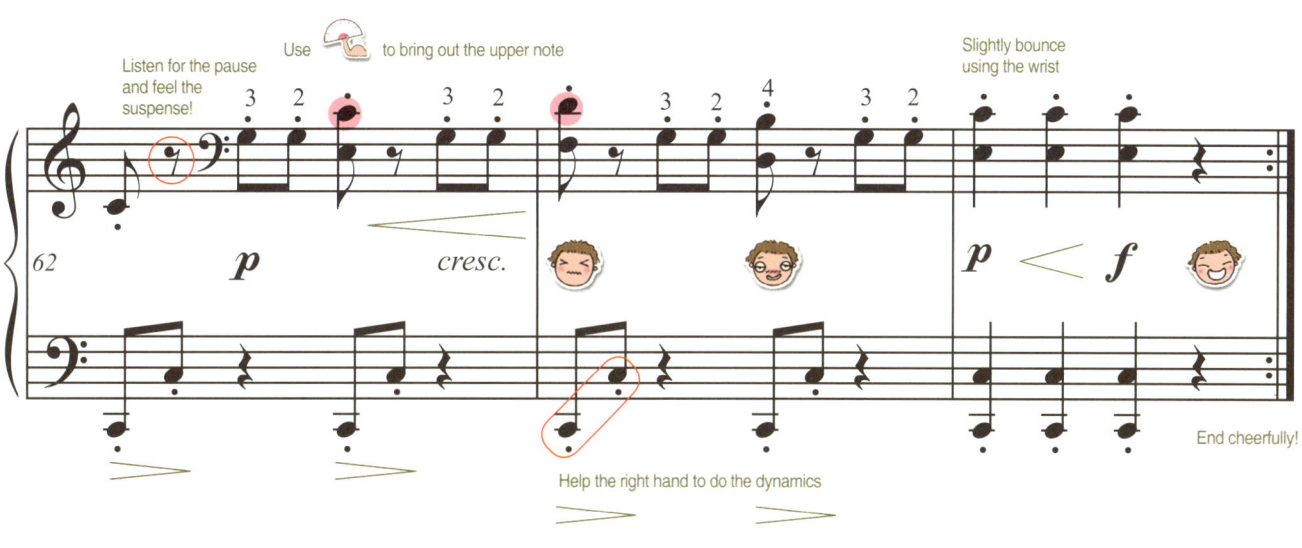

M. Clementi Sonatine

Op. 36 No. 4 in F Major, 1st Movement

Ms. Silverplate's Smart Tips

❁ **How do I keep my thumb from being clumsy?**

Let's learn the secret of the thumb!

🍀 Keeping a good posture is important especially in fast passages!
The thumb must maintain its poise and the U-shape.

🍀 As soon as you hit the key, let the thumb graze the key as if a fish quivers vigorously.

🍀 Keep your ears active! Listen carefully before and after the notes in order to connect them well.

> **Learn that term!** **What is a U-shape?**
> The U-shape refers to a concept introduced on p.43 of *Nine Gifts from a Piano Teacher* written by Dr. Joy Song.
> It's a shape that should be created and maintained between the thumb and the index finger.

❁ **Could you show me an example of the clumsy thumb?**

🍀 In the above passage, play the highlighted "columns," the skeletal structure of the passage, and let your ears learn the harmonic progression.

🍀 Express the dissonant chords 😐 resolving into consonant ones 🙂 .
(The reason the consonant chord in m. 39 isn't a happy face is that it hasn't resolved into the tonic yet.)

🍀 If you want to play faster, group notes into 4 or 8. Let the first note of each group create momentum for rest of the notes.

M. Clementi Op. 36 No. 4, 1st movt.

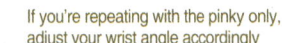
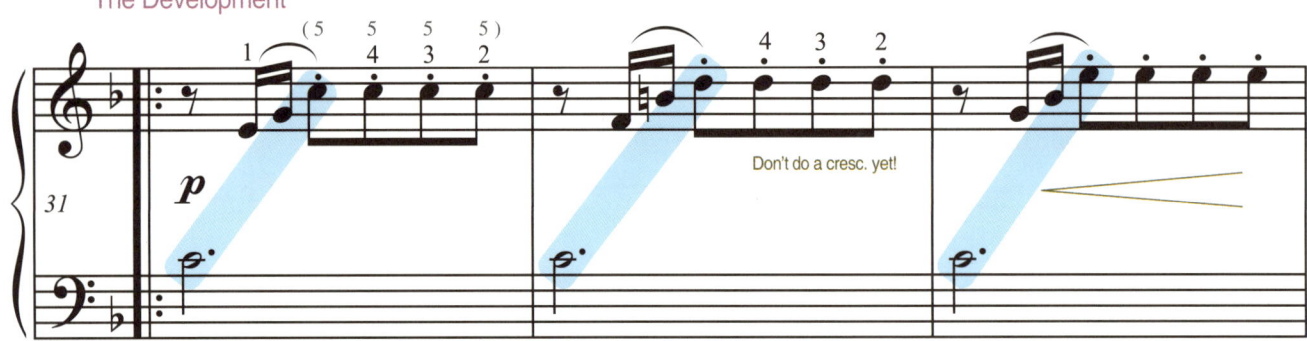
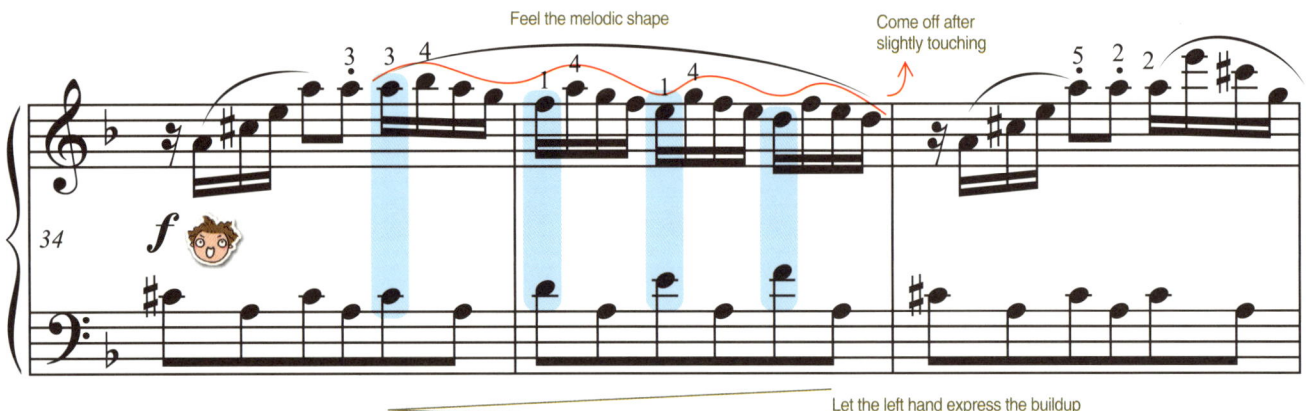

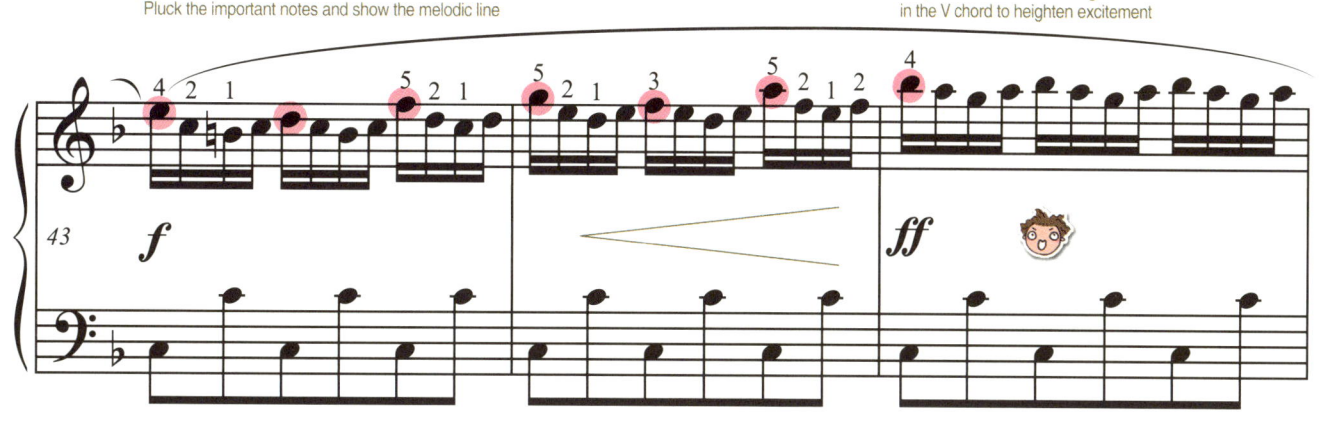
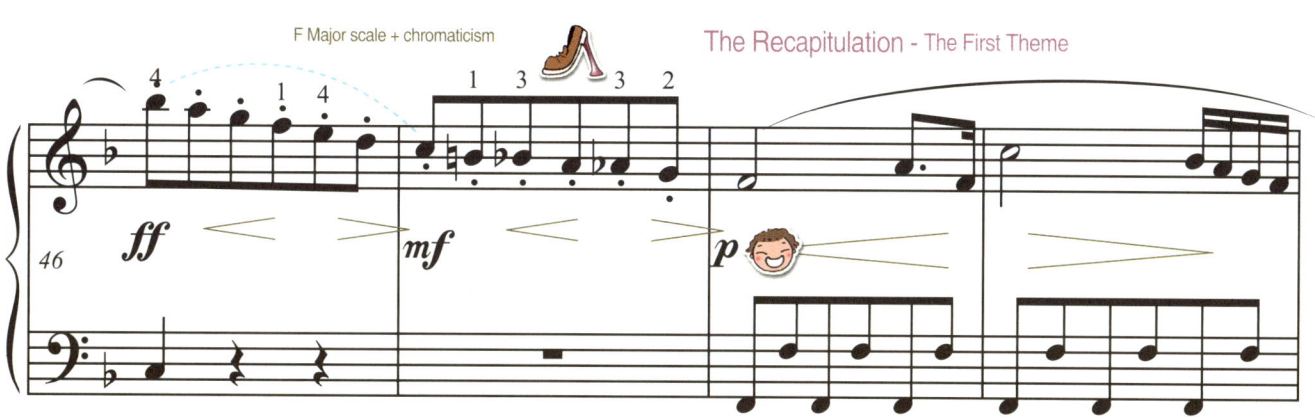
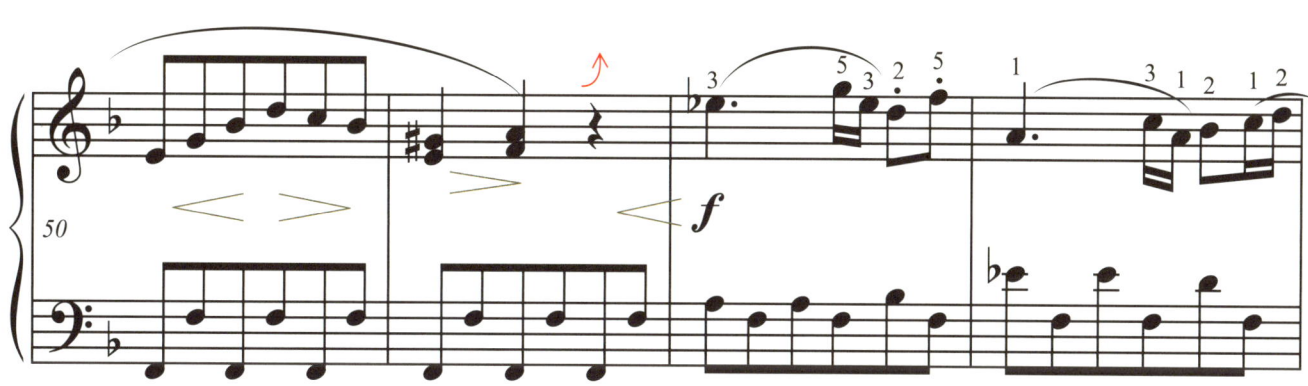
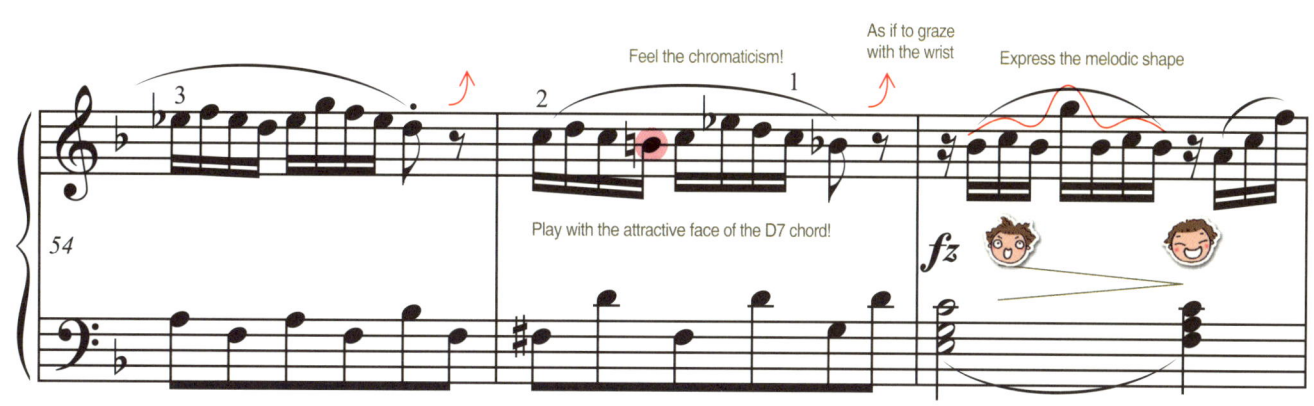

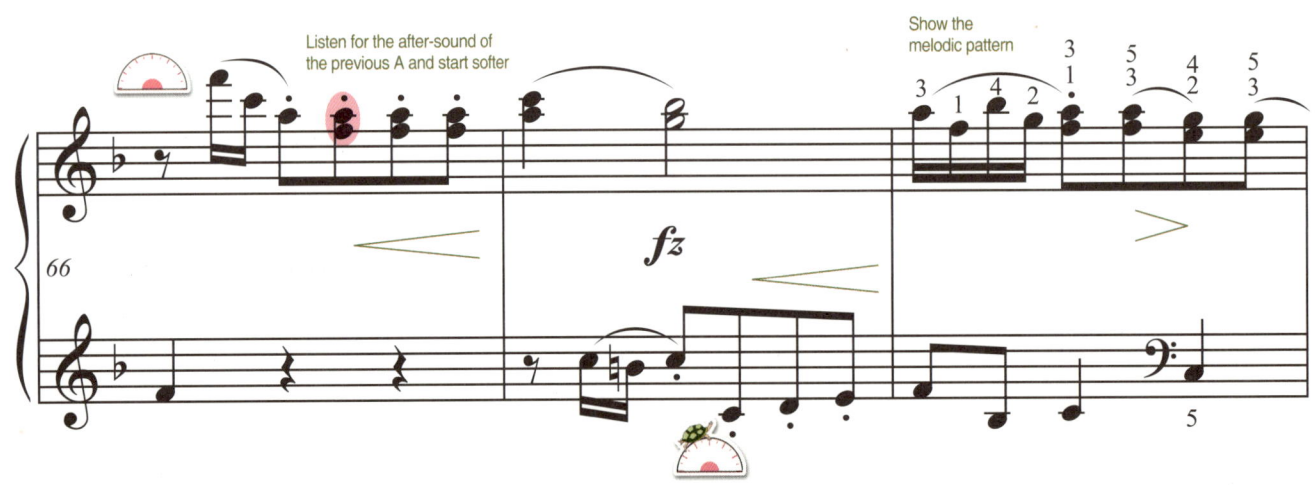

The Coda

Kuhlau Sonatine

Op. 20 No. 1 in C Major, 1st Movement

Ms. Silverplate's Smart Tips

❊ How can I make my right hand sound great without being too loud?

🌀 First, play the first note G, listen for it fade, and then play the following interval (C and E) softer; mix it into the reverberation of G.

🌀 For better balance, apply more arm weight on the left-hand melody line.

🌀 Use legato pedal as shown above.

❊ How can I make the lyrical second theme more beautiful?

🌀 A complete change of scenes!
As you finish off m. 16, imagine the echo of the first note of the second theme, B.

🌀 Sing out each note abundantly, as if you are an opera singer.
Make the chromaticism in mm. 18 and 19 sound sticky.

🌀 Think of the characteristic and appropriate angling of each finger, and apply more arm weight.

Kuhlau Op. 20 No. 1, 1st movt.

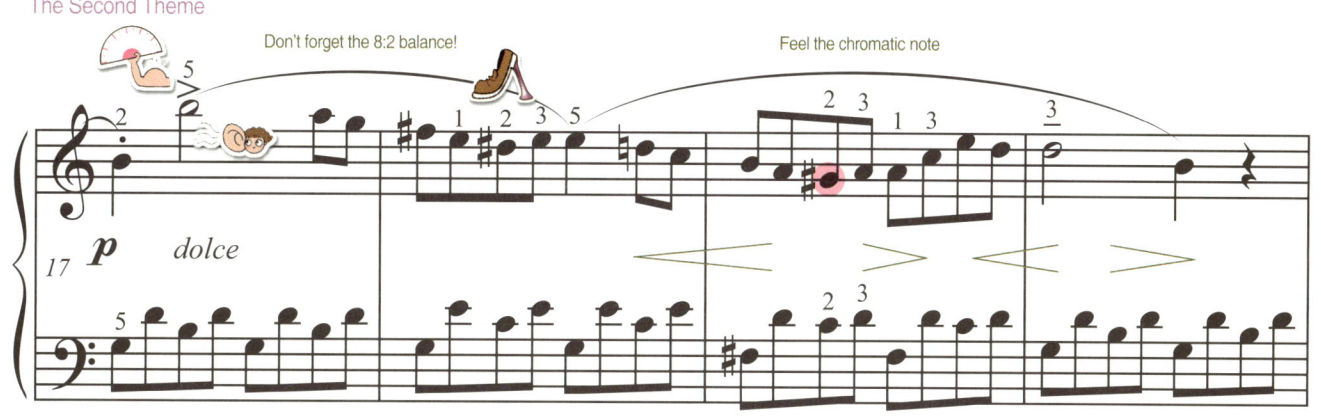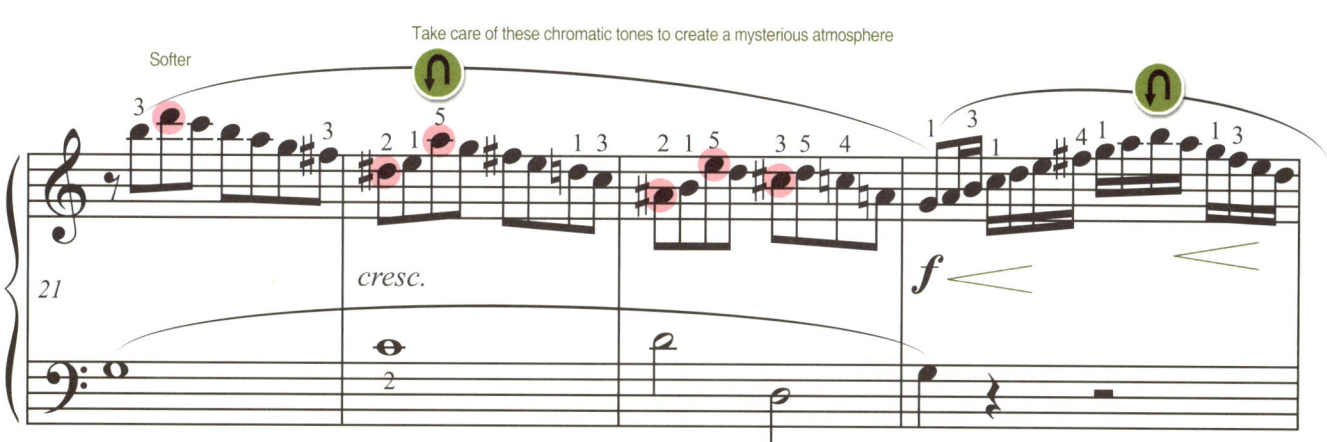

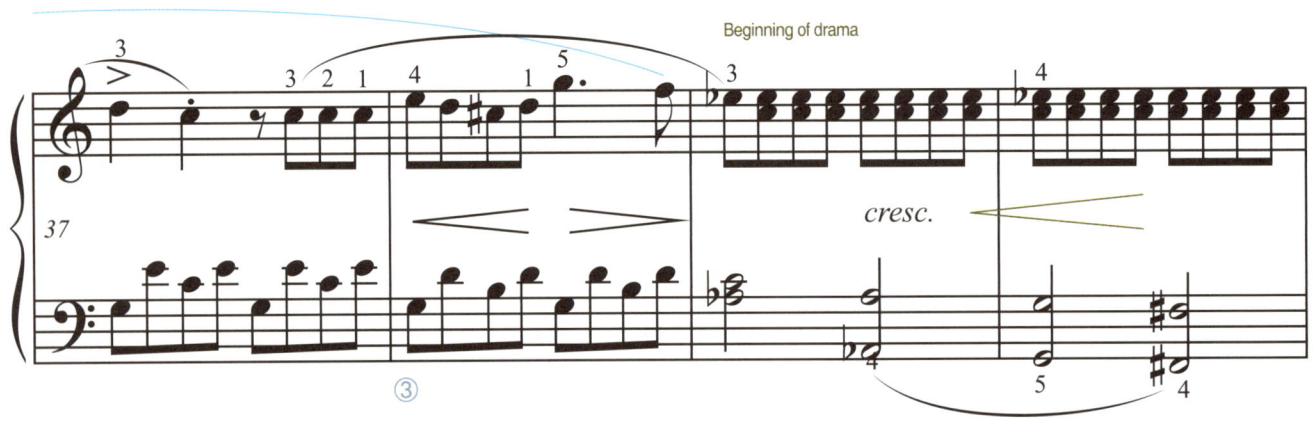
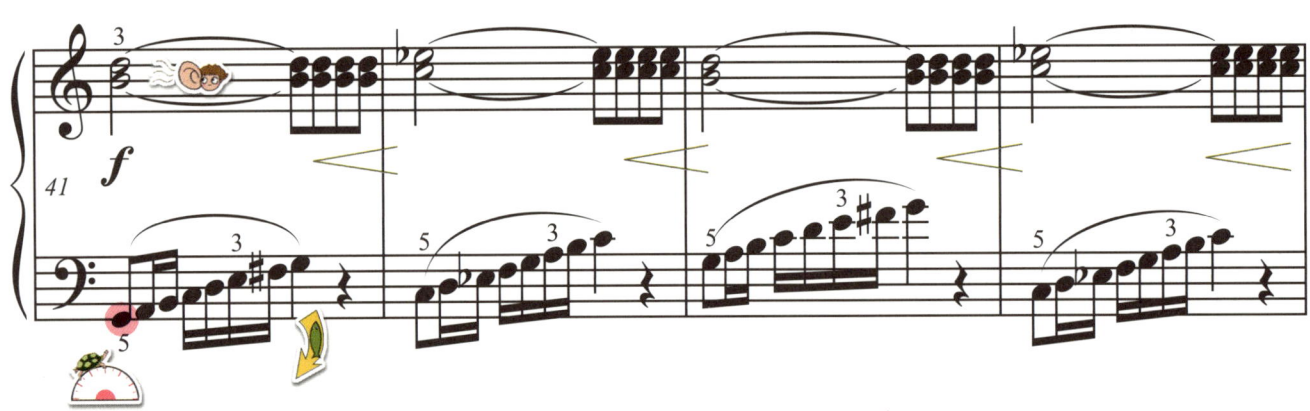

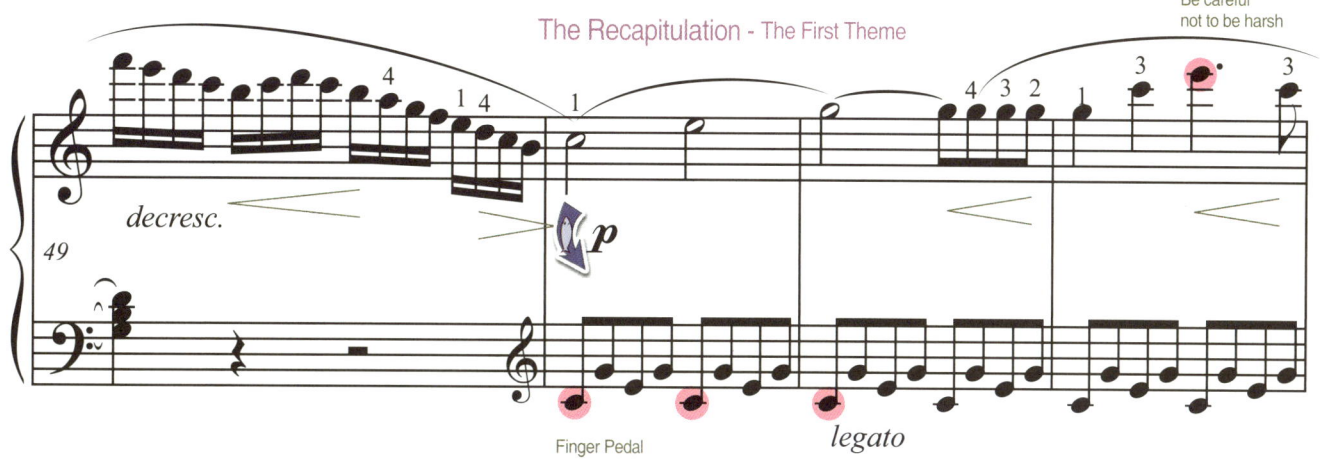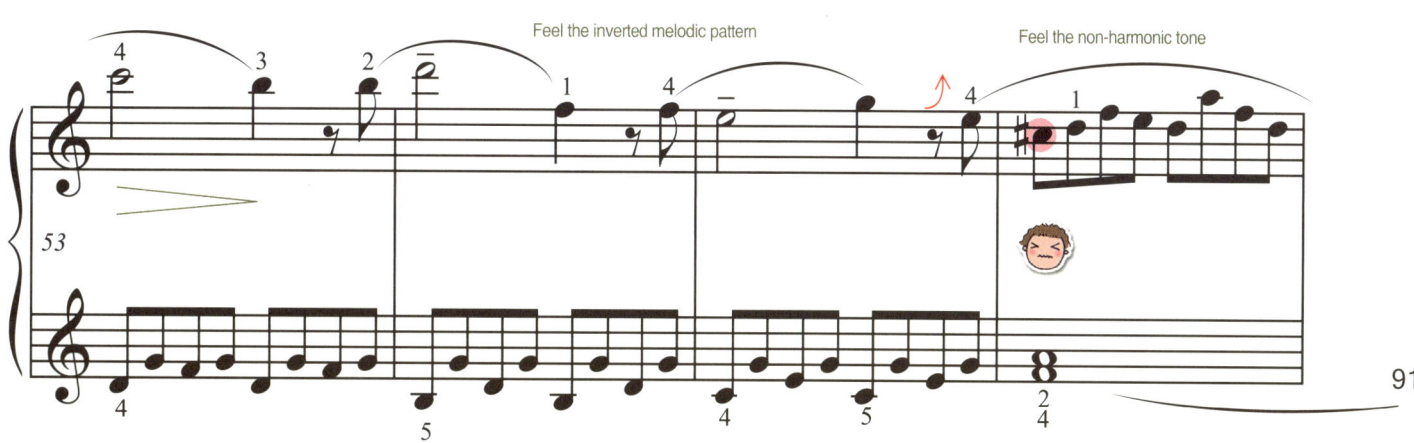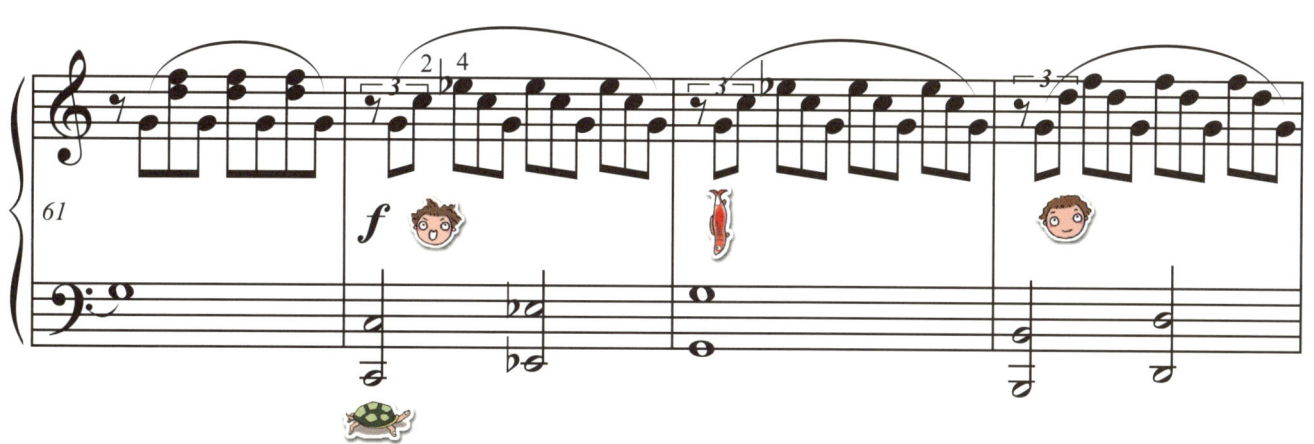

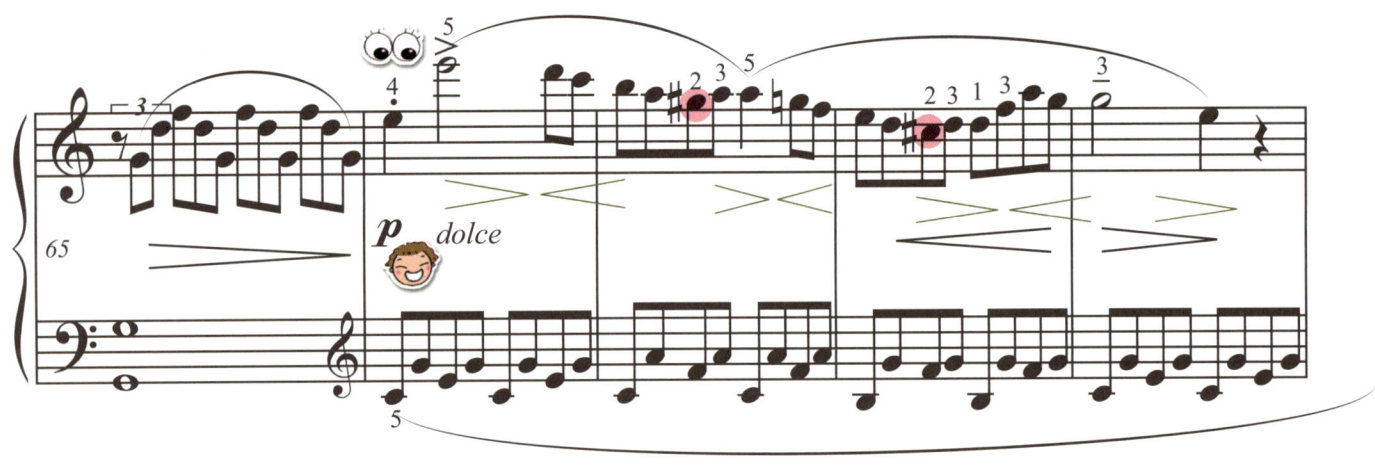

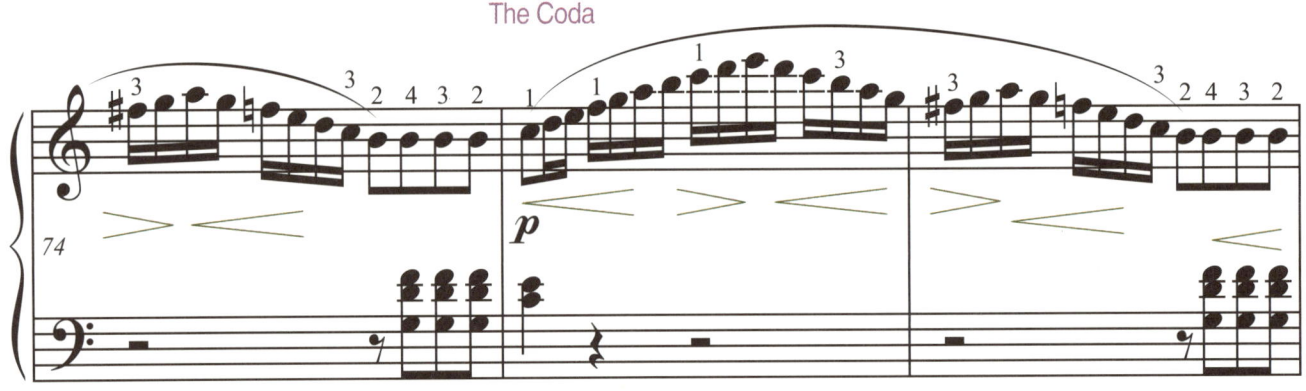

Meno

Kuhlau Sonatine

Op. 20 No. 1 in F Major, 2nd Movement

Ms. Silverplate's Smart Tips

🌼 **The dotted rhythm figure with thirds is really awkward. What should I do?**

🌀 Use the interosseous muscles to pinch.

🌀 Maintain the shape of a turtle shell, and play the notes after the first one of the phrase
as if you're just gently touching them (be close to the keys!).
As you do this, try keeping the shape of your hand intact.

🌀 For an elegant finish, raise your wrist gently on the last note of the group.

· **You want to make it sound even better?**
Try playing the dotted note longer and the shorter note even shorter.

[Name that term] **interosseous muscles**
Interosseous muscles are used to spread out your fingers. They are located
between your knuckles and your wrist, and they are attached to each one of your fingers.
If you use these muscles well, you will be able to move your fingers more freely
and to play intervals and chords more precisely.

🌼 **How can I use the pedal better?**

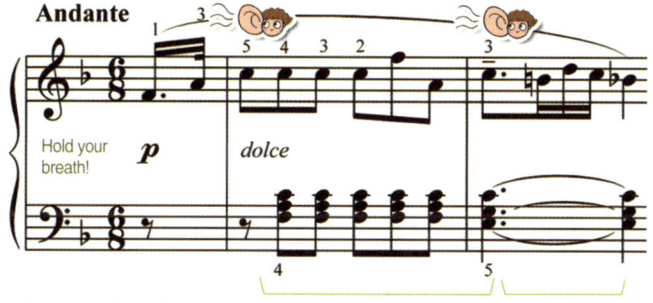

Here's the perfect chance to witness the effects of the "after-pedal" technique.
Let's train your ears and get rid of those messy after-sounds!

🌀 Play C in the right hand in the first measure, and listen for its fading.

🌀 As you're listening for the trail of C, press the pedal.

🌀 How to change the pedal cleanly at each harmony change:
Repeat the above procedure for the 2nd measure –
play the first note, C, listen for it and change the pedal.

Kuhlau Op. 20 No. 1, 2nd movt.

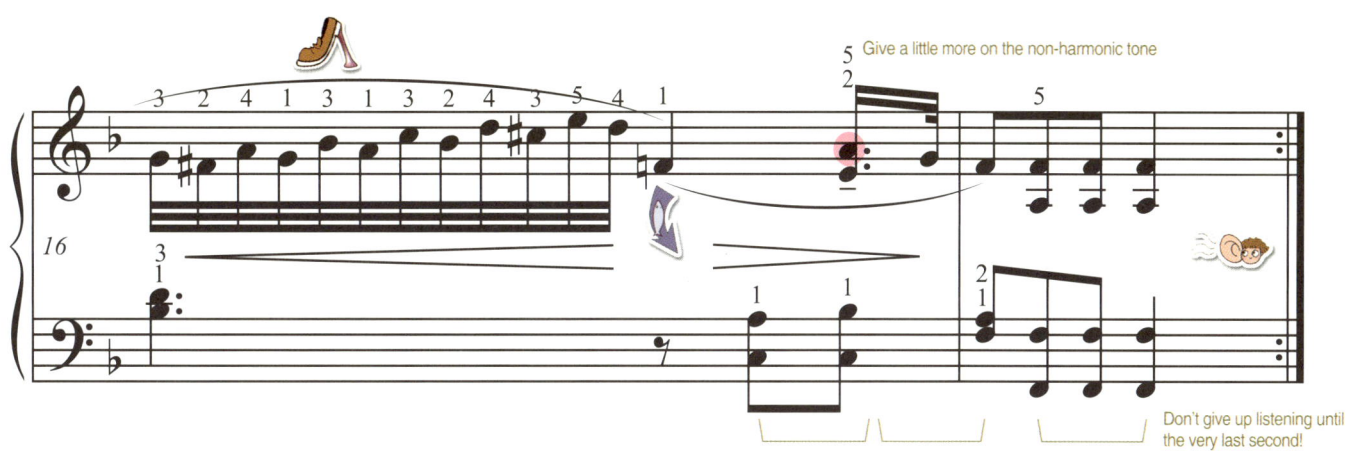

Sonatine **Story**

Ms. Silverplate interviewed Miss Nuance

Silverplate : Hi, Miss Nuance! Nice to meet you!

Nuance : (smiles) Yes, pleasure to meet you.

Silverplate : You are incredibly popular these days in the music world. Can you tell us your secret?

Nuance : Well, I wouldn't say it's a secret really. I guess it's important to play a melody naturally, as if you're talking with somebody.

Silverplate : As if you're talking? What do you mean?

Nuance : Well, think about it. When you're small, you start out with saying shorter sentences. You start with saying "mom" or "mamma" and then as you grow up you can start to say longer things like, "mom, I want to eat a sandwich."

Silverplate : Well, yes.

Nuance : What we mean by nuance is that you notice all these smaller motivic units that make up a bigger phrase, and flavor each of those units. When you do that, a long phrase can take on elegant shapes. Just like your voice rises and falls when you talk.

Silverplate : Hm… it's a bit difficult to understand.

Nuance : Well, just try saying something, and you'll see. Don't things go up and down slightly, as you speak? Listen for this intonation. Now imagine that you don't have intonation in speech. What you're saying becomes immediately monotonous. It's exactly the same in music.

Silverplate : Oh, you're right! I guess you also mean that there's nothing more musical than just being natural. Thank you for joining us today, Miss Nuance, and for teaching us how to make our music sound more elegant!

Sonatine Story

❁ **Imagine fragrance in music! And show it subtly!**

M. Clementi Op. 36 No. 4, Movt. I

M. Clementi Op. 36 No. 3, Movt. I

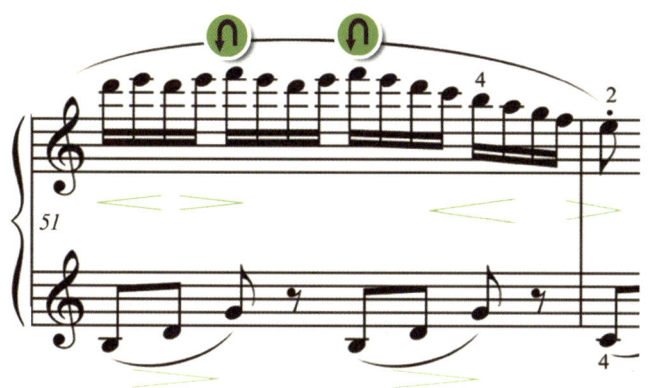

Kuhlau Op. 20 No. 1, Movt. III

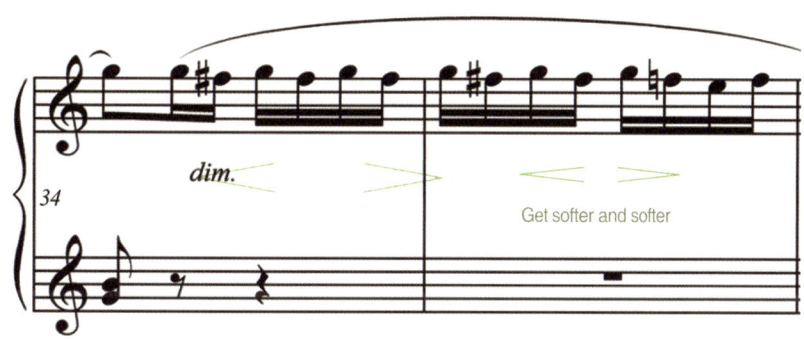

Get softer and softer

Kuhlau Op. 20 No. 1, Movt. III

Kuhlau Sonatine

Op. 20 No. 1 in C Major, 3rd Movement

Ms. Silverplate's Smart Tips

🌼 **How should I play the patterns that repeat over and over?**

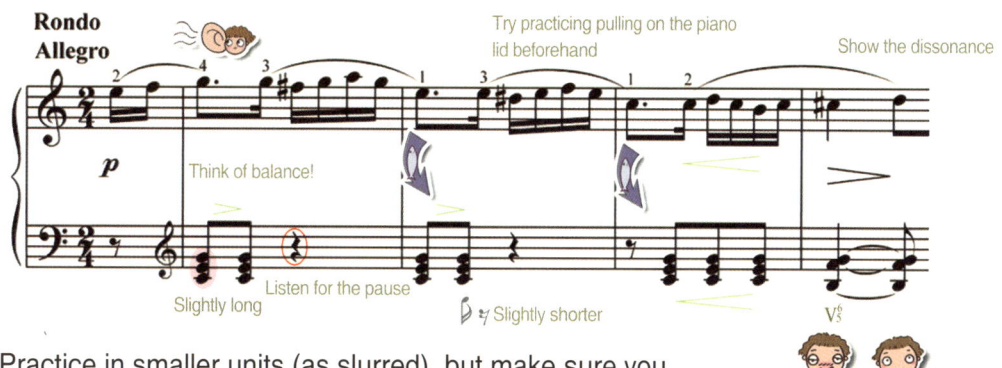

- Practice in smaller units (as slurred), but make sure you pull out each note to produce a firm sound.

- Give nuance to each slurred unit!

- It would also be nice for the left hand to do a slight crescendo toward the V_5^6 harmony.

🌼 **What should I do with those really long scales?**

Don't be scared with long scales. If you know where to put stress and to release, everything will go smoothly.

- Recognize all those scales that appear from time to time, and then figure out how to give nuance to each of those. (Refer to *Pearl's Secrets to Scales* Vol. 5)

- If you stress the V^7 chord and then resolve to I chord, you can unearth the skeletal structure of the piece, and your playing will sound better.

Kuhlau Op. 20 No. 1, 3rd movt.

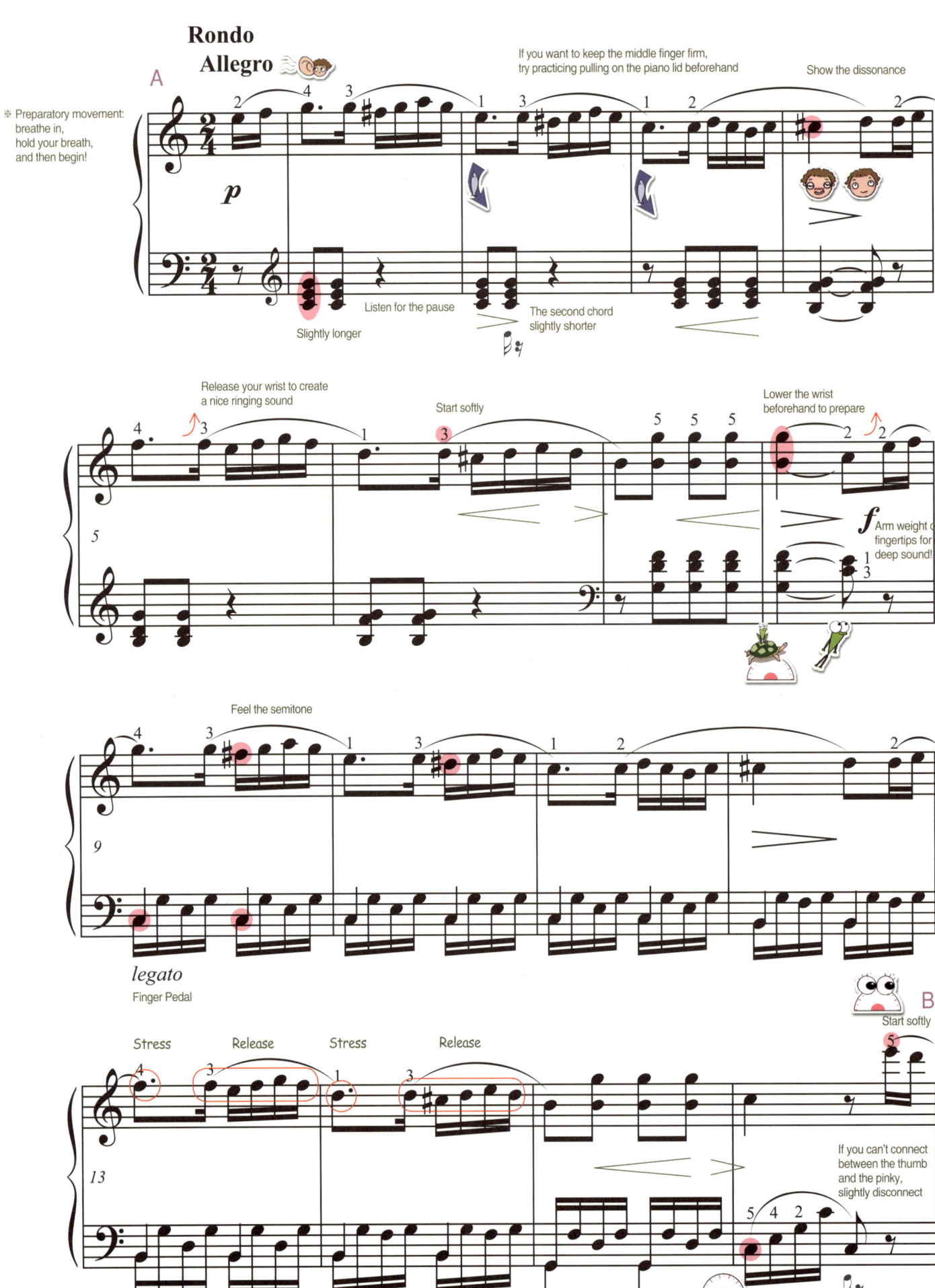

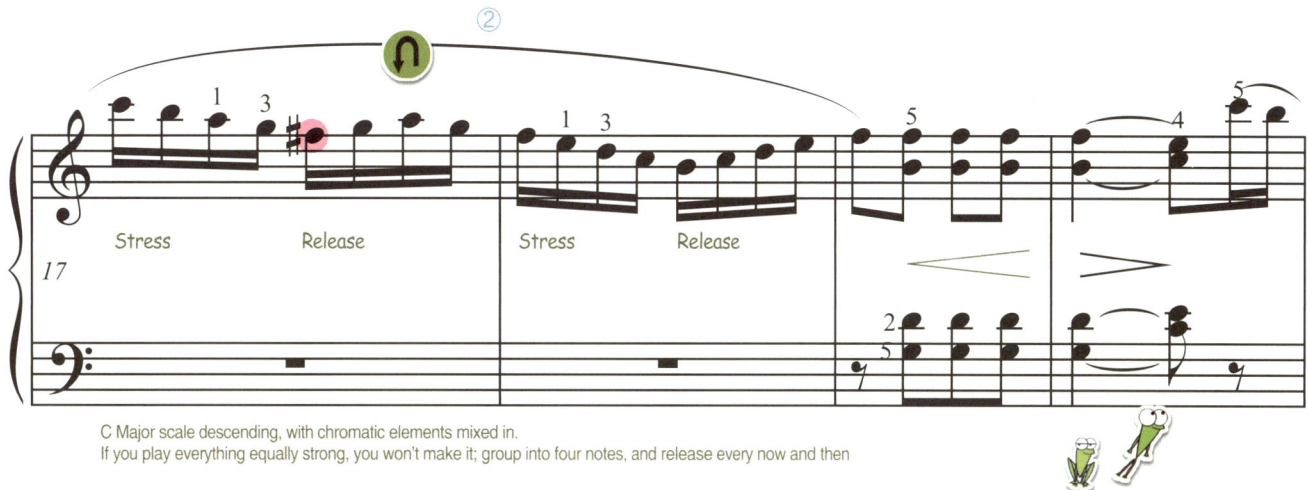

C Major scale descending, with chromatic elements mixed in.
If you play everything equally strong, you won't make it; group into four notes, and release every now and then

In 25 ~ 32 , the phrase is long, so group into 8 notes and stress + release.
Your hand shape and angle should be intact, and your wrist has to be flexible.

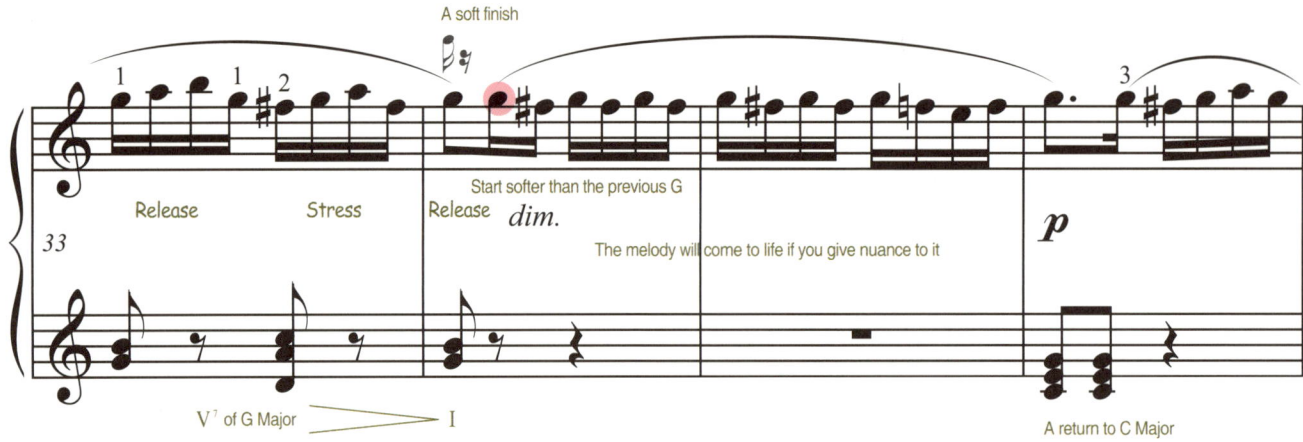

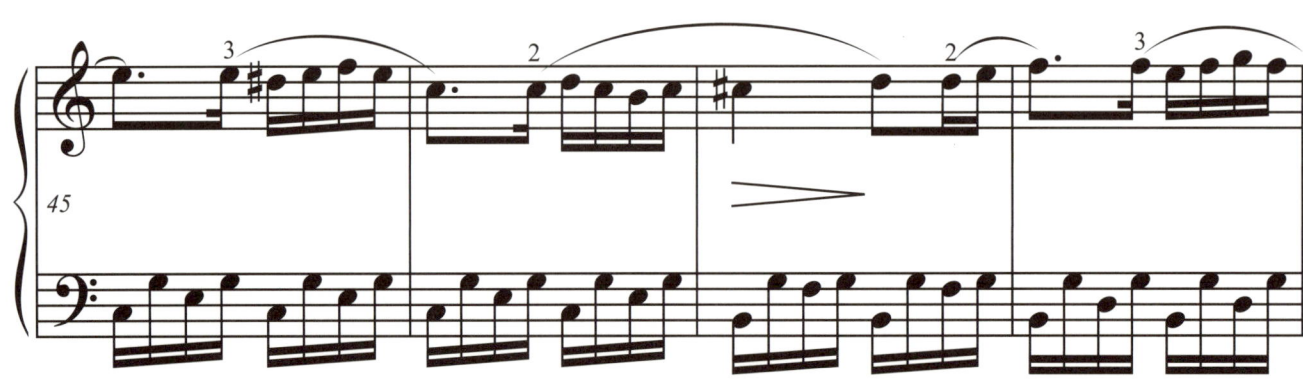

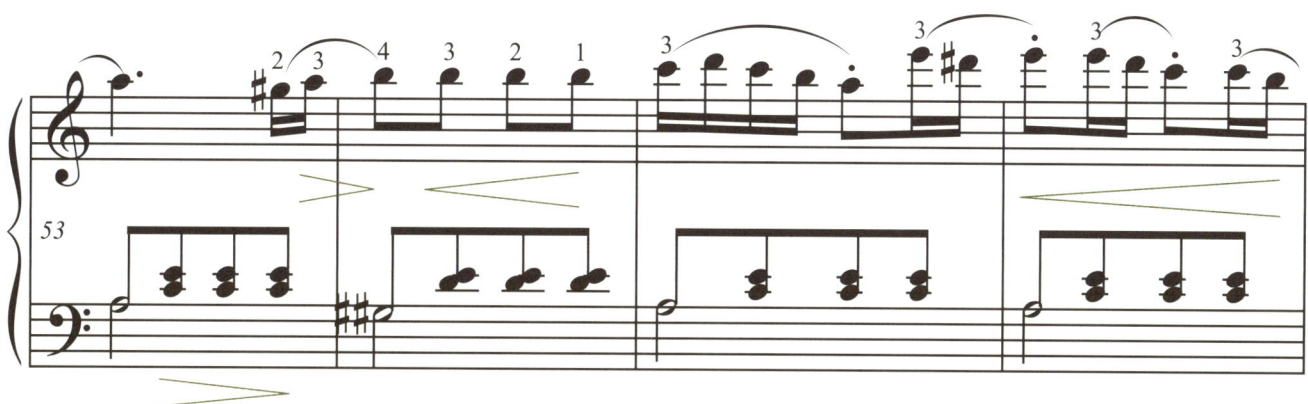

105

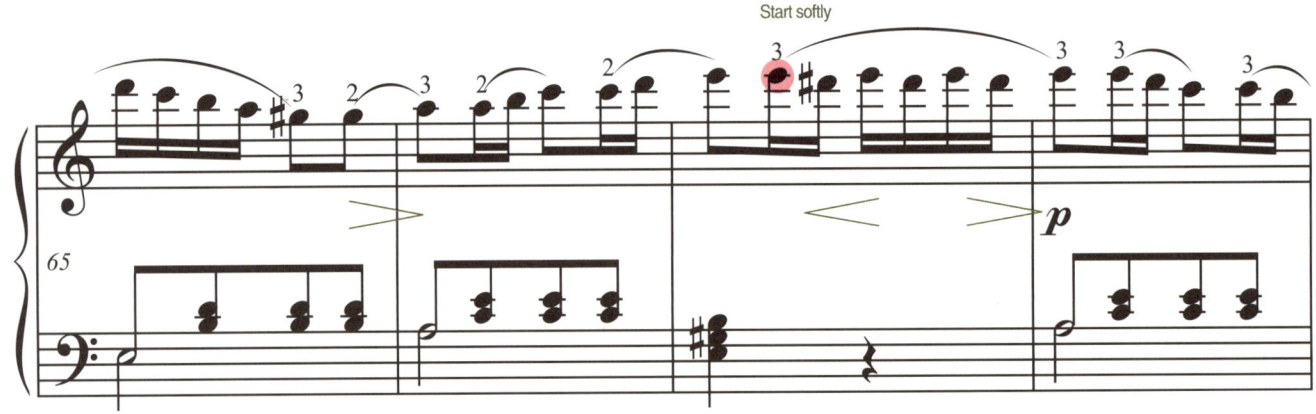
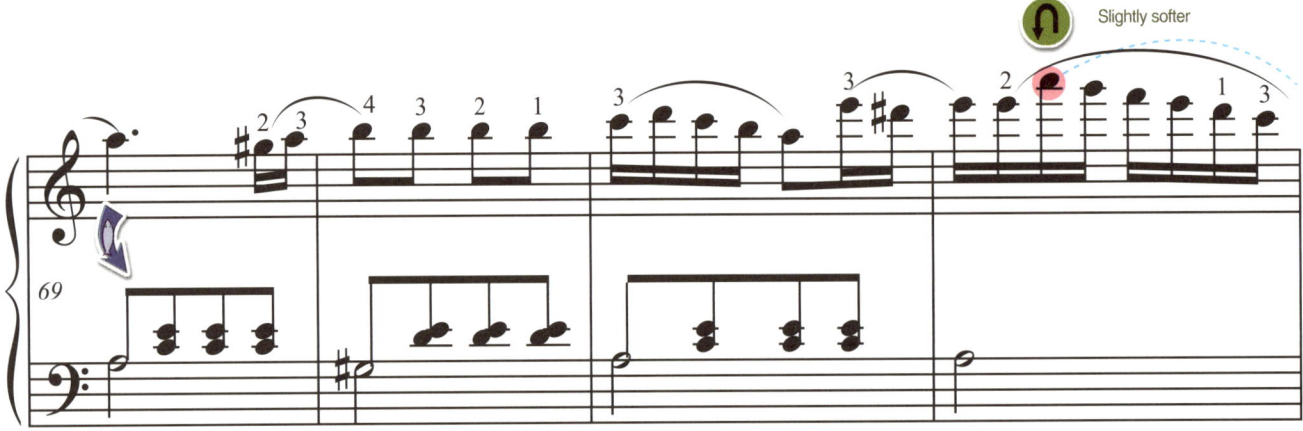
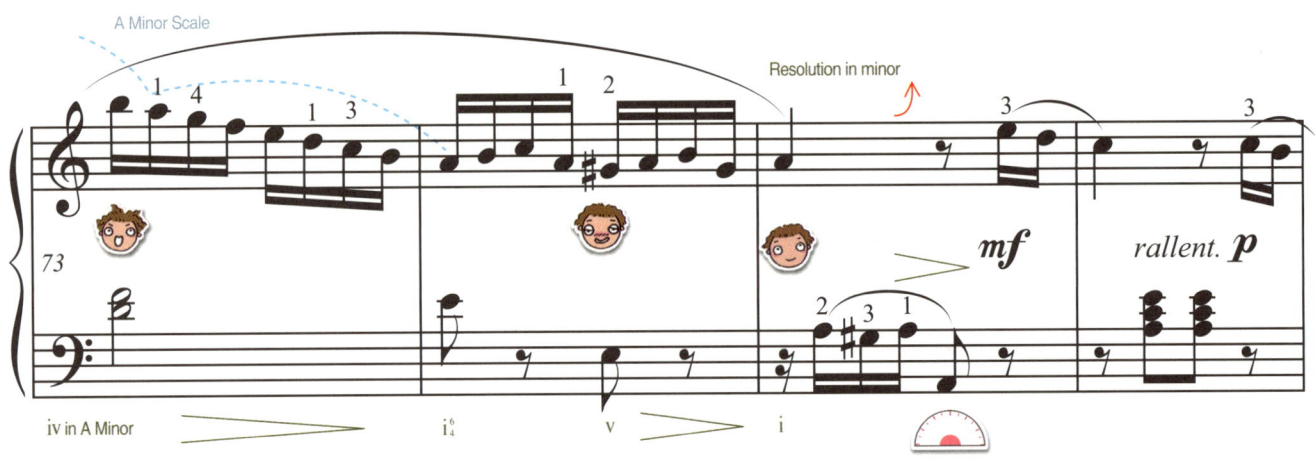
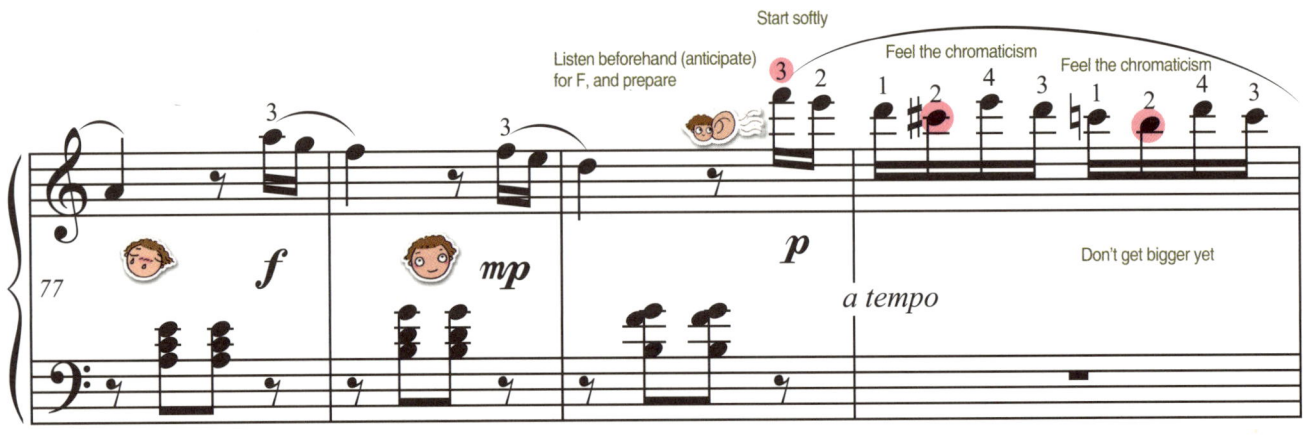

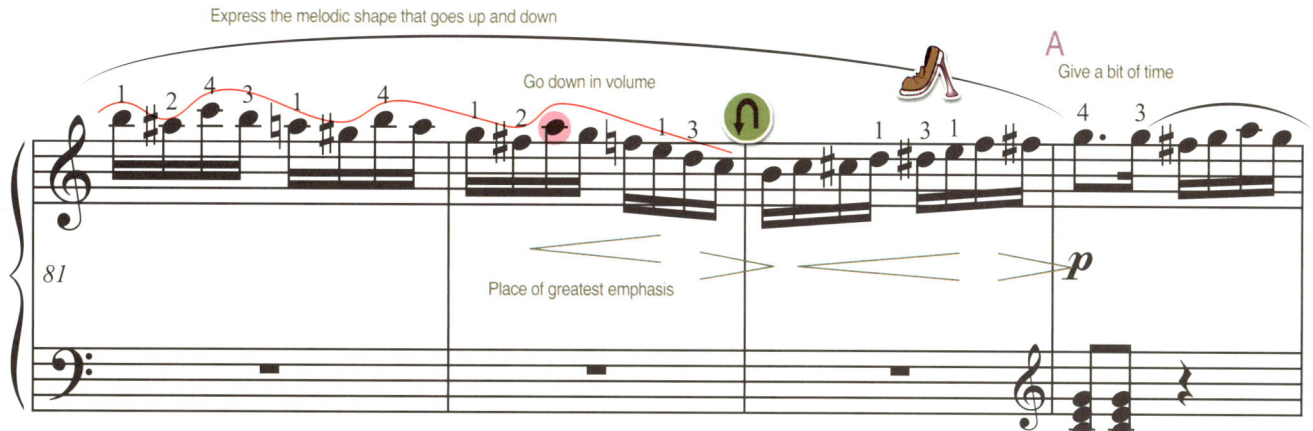

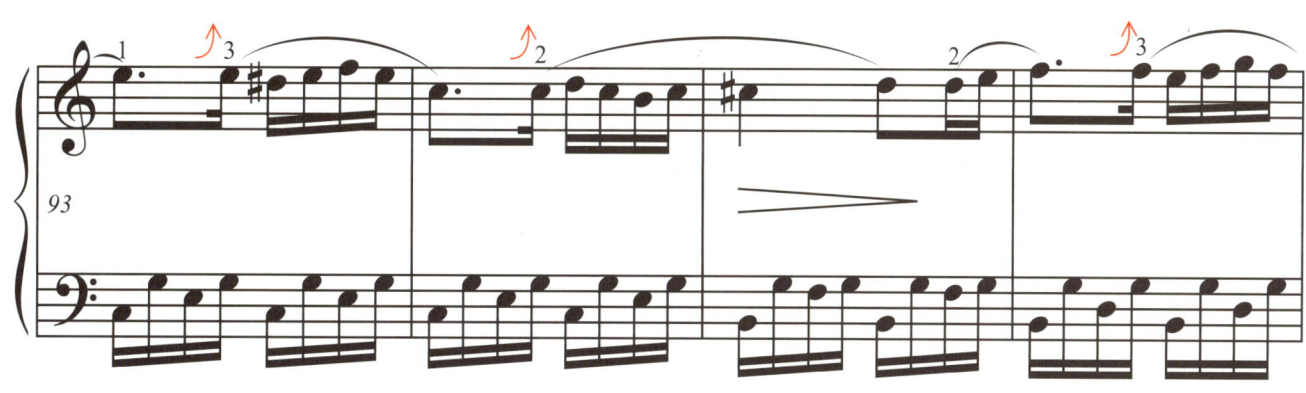

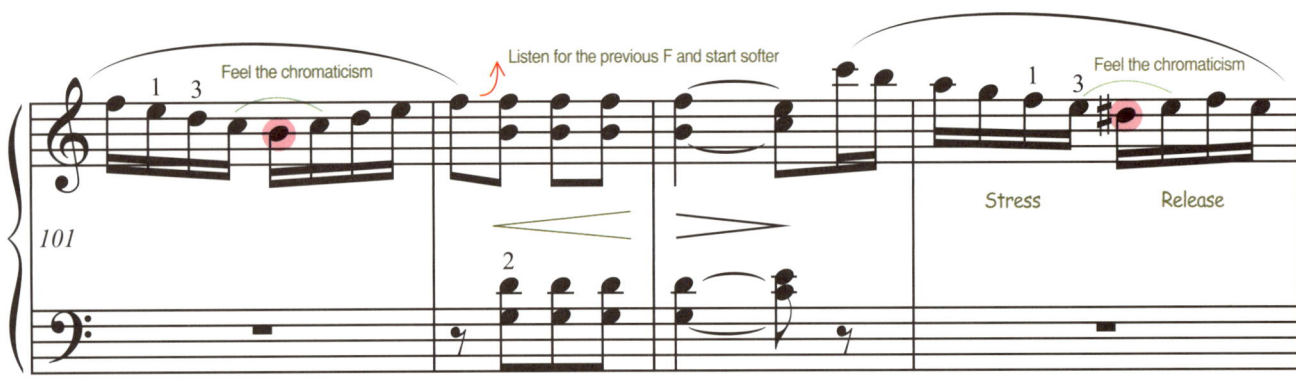
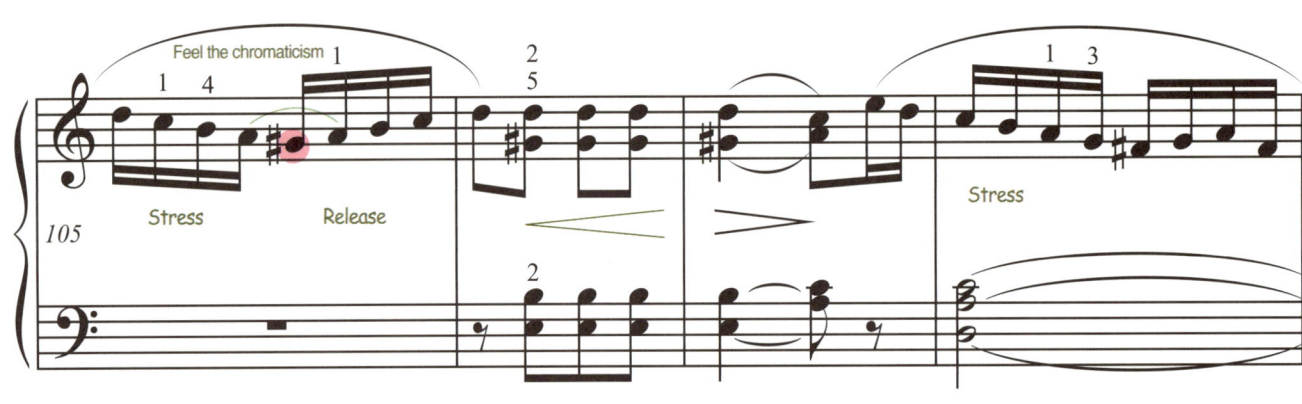
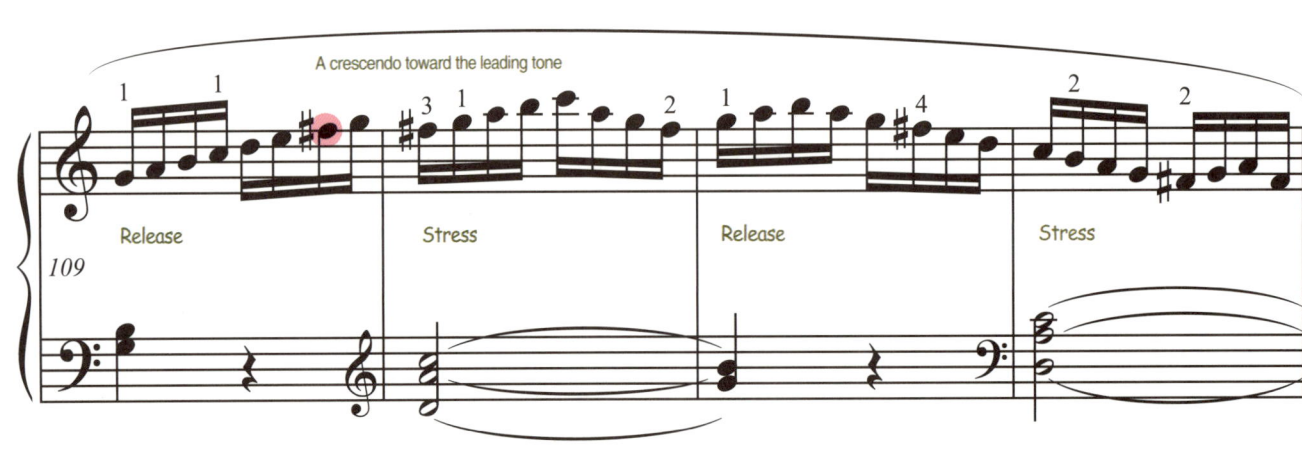

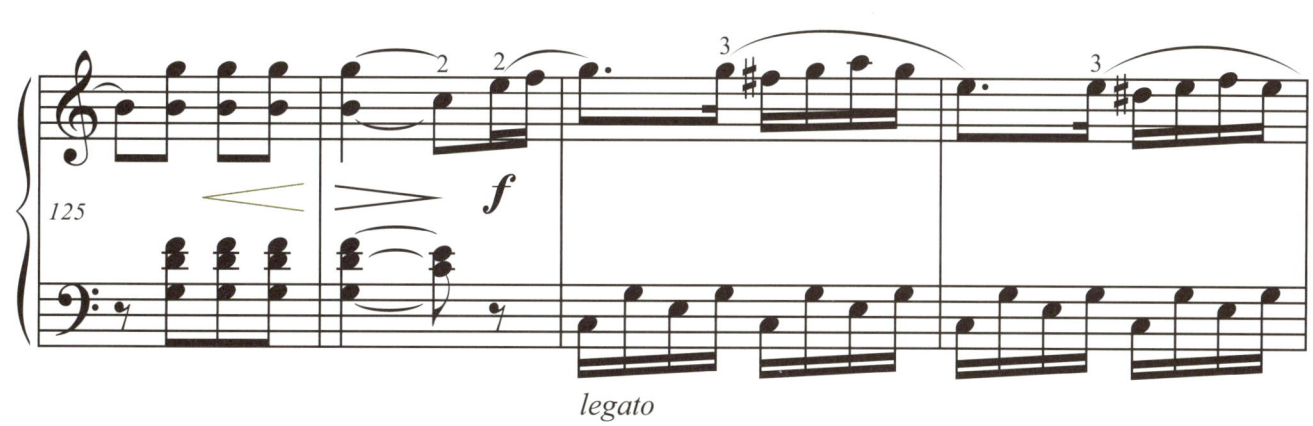

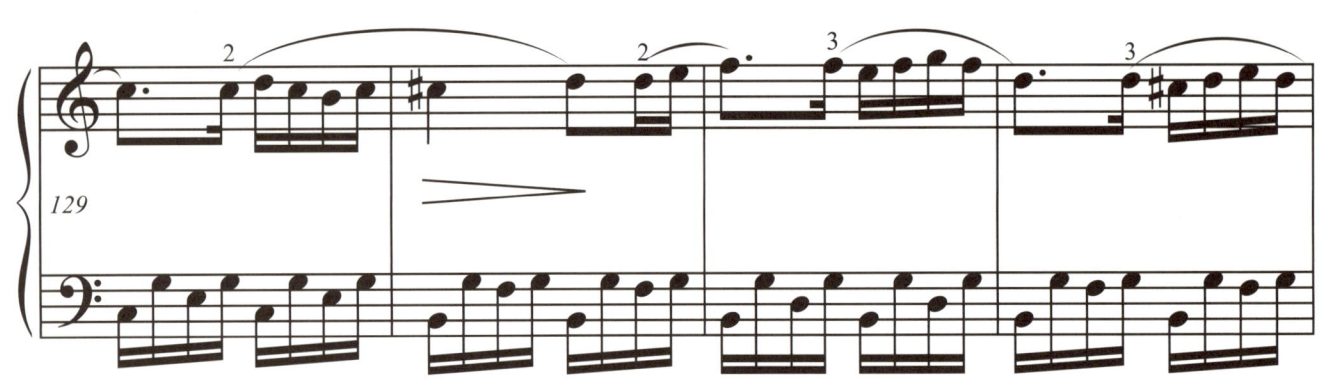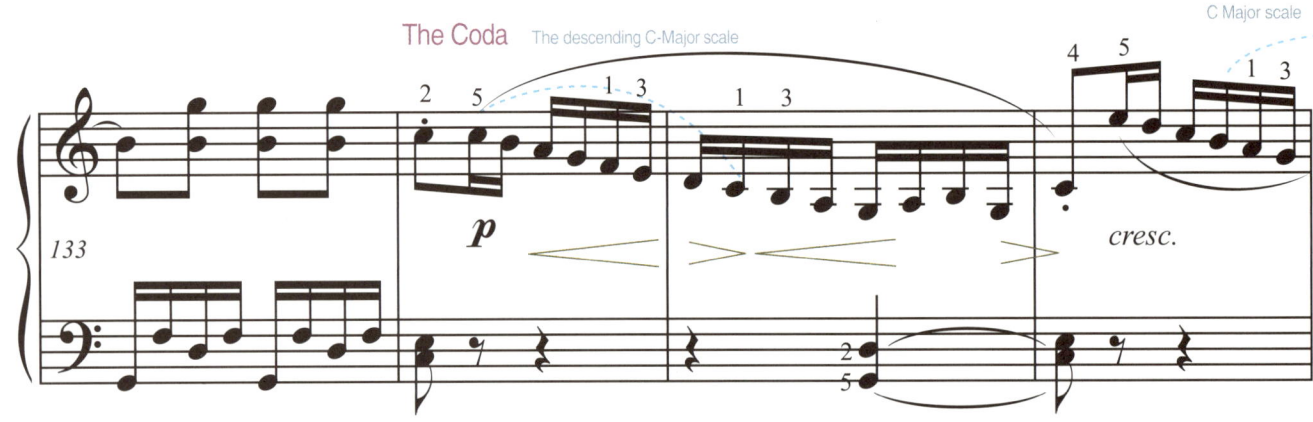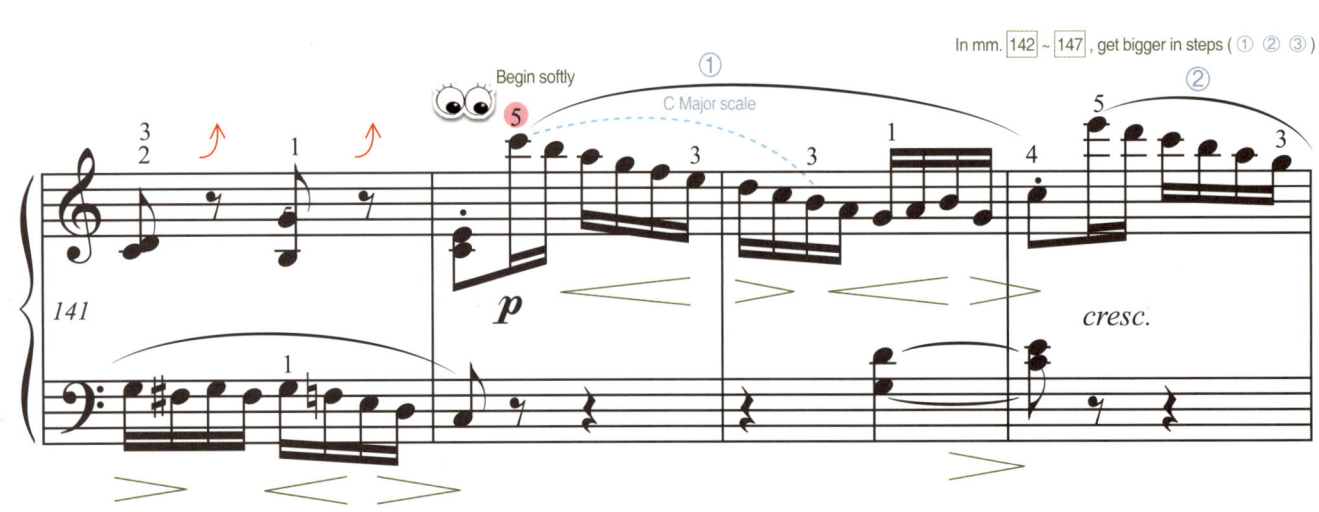

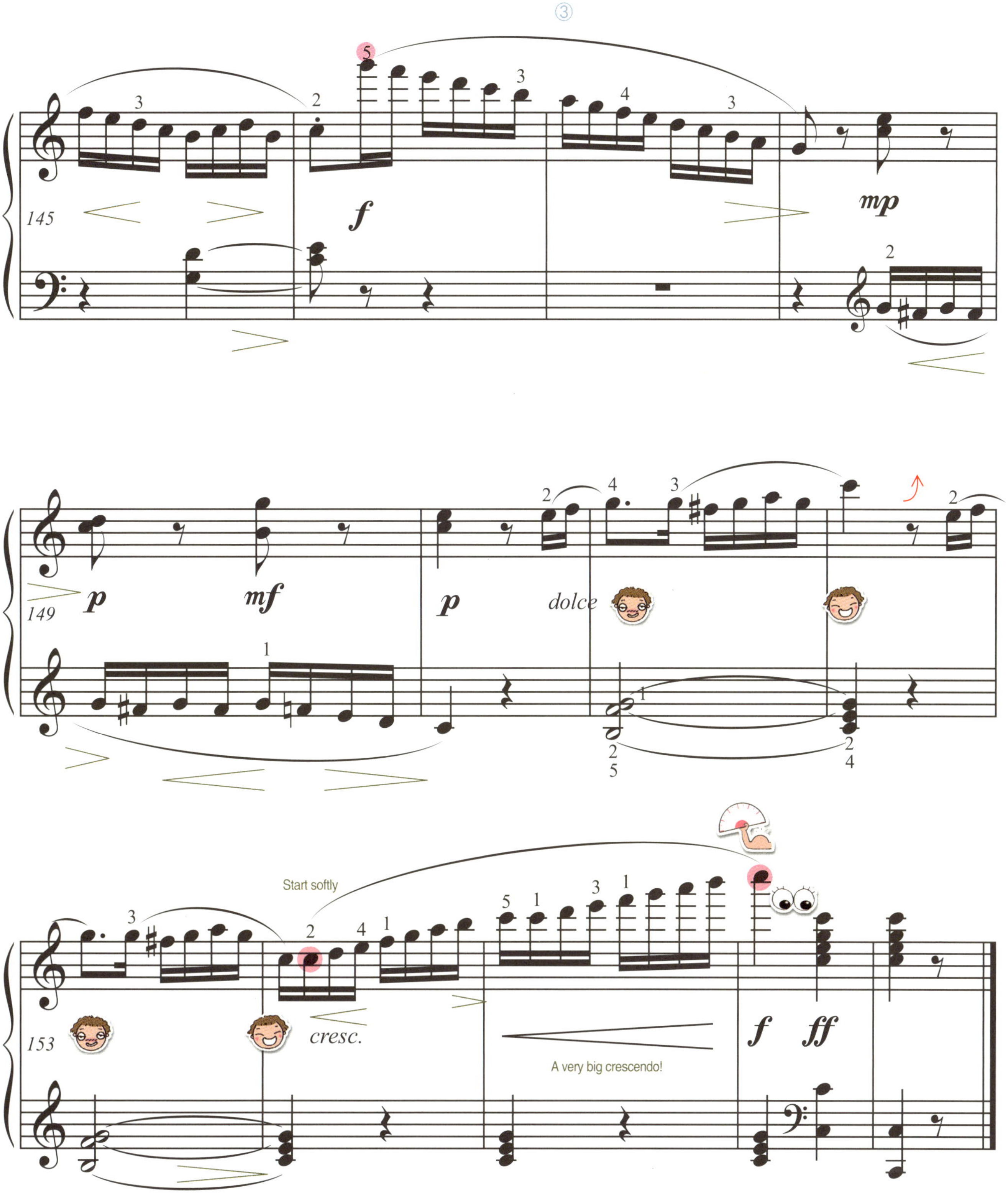
③
145
f
mp
149
p
mf
p
dolce
153
Start softly
cresc.
A very big crescendo!
f
ff

Kuhlau Sonatine

Op. 55 No. 2 in G Major, 1st Movement

Ms. Silverplate's Smart Tips

🌼 **It's difficult sometimes to go in one breath!**

Make sure to listen to the echo, after a long note within a melody line!

Playing 8 measures in one breath needs practicing

Play the left hand without making any sound - this will help you reduce the volume of the accompaniment

Feel the chromaticism

© Don't worry - let's practice it! Before playing, try singing the melody line.

If you can sing 4 measures in one breath, it's already a success.

Some people can even manage to sing 8 measures in one breath.

Why don't you try it as well?

🌼 **How can I play the scales tastefully?**

Get bigger toward the leading tone

Do a crescendo toward the leading tone

Change of atmosphere

Listen to the pause!

In *p*, it's more effective almost not to do the <>

Shall we express the beauty of all those colorful scales?

© Name that scale! Check 🐢 .

© As you move from the middle finger to the thumb, maintain the U-shape in the thumb area and move on smoothly. (Refer to Vol. 5 of the *Pearl's Scale Secrets*)

Kuhlau Op. 55 No. 2, 1st movt.

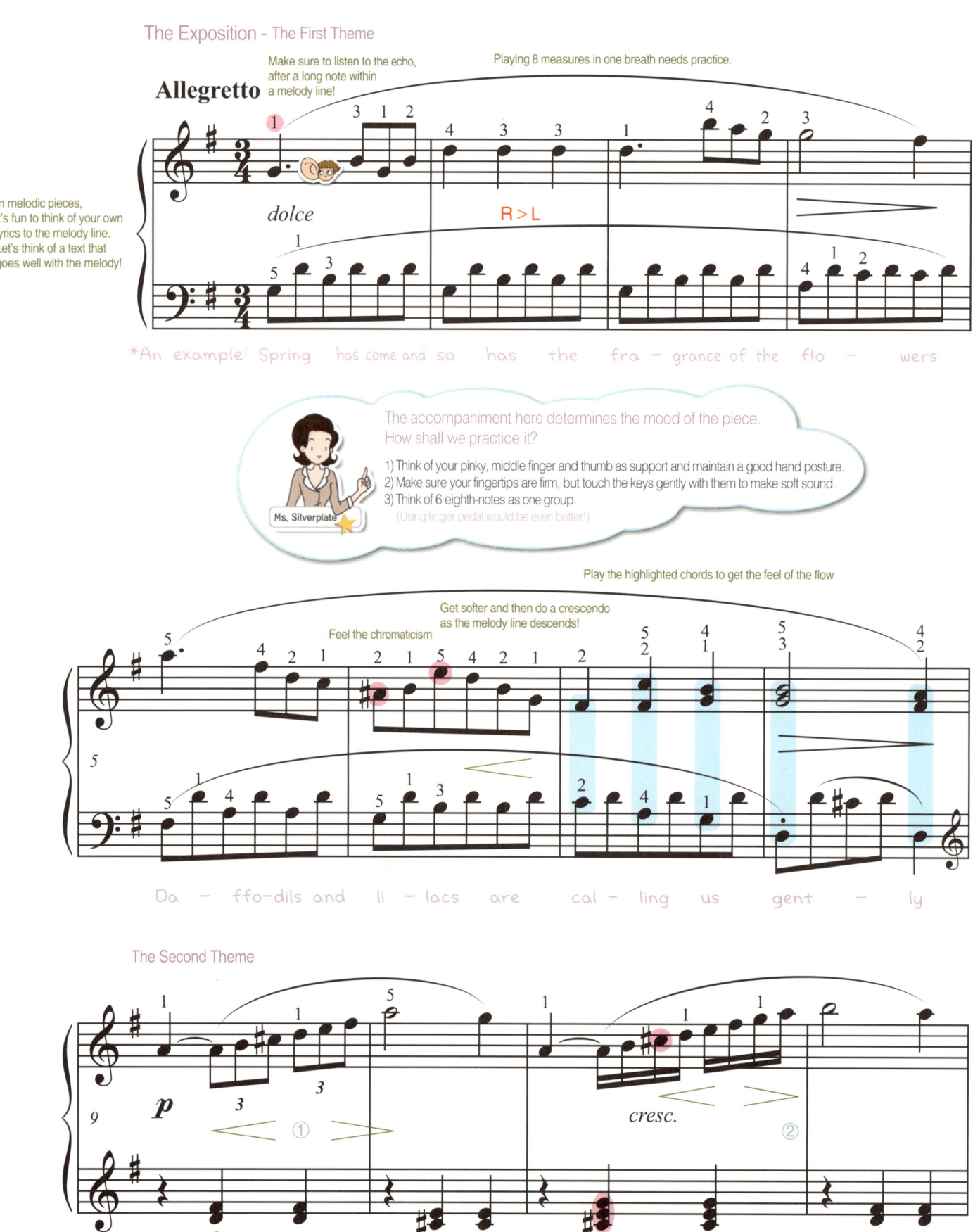

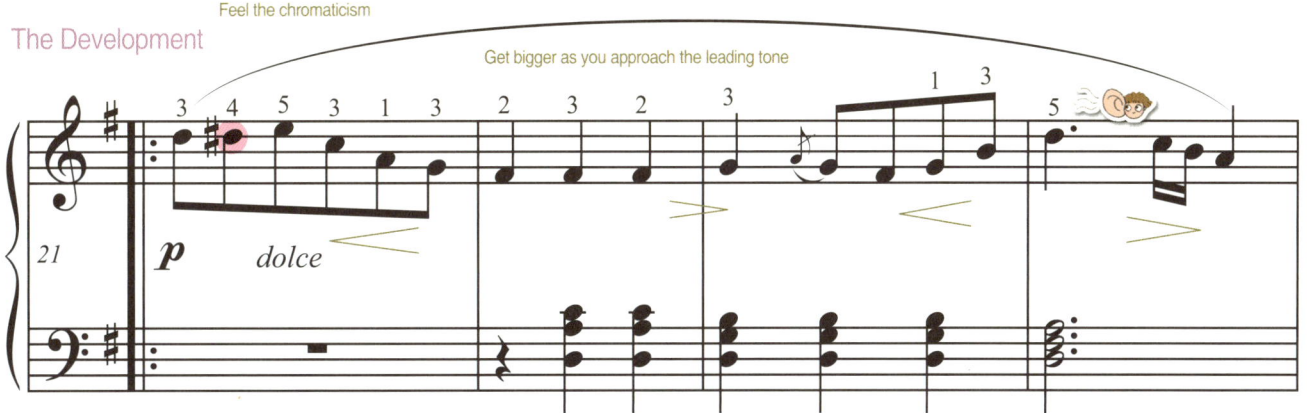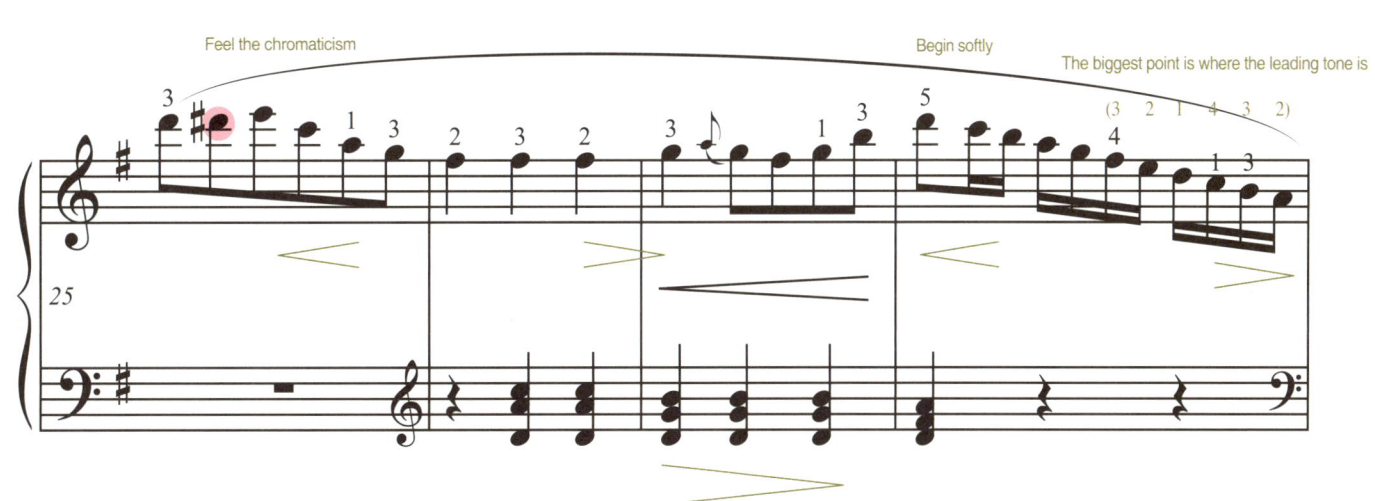

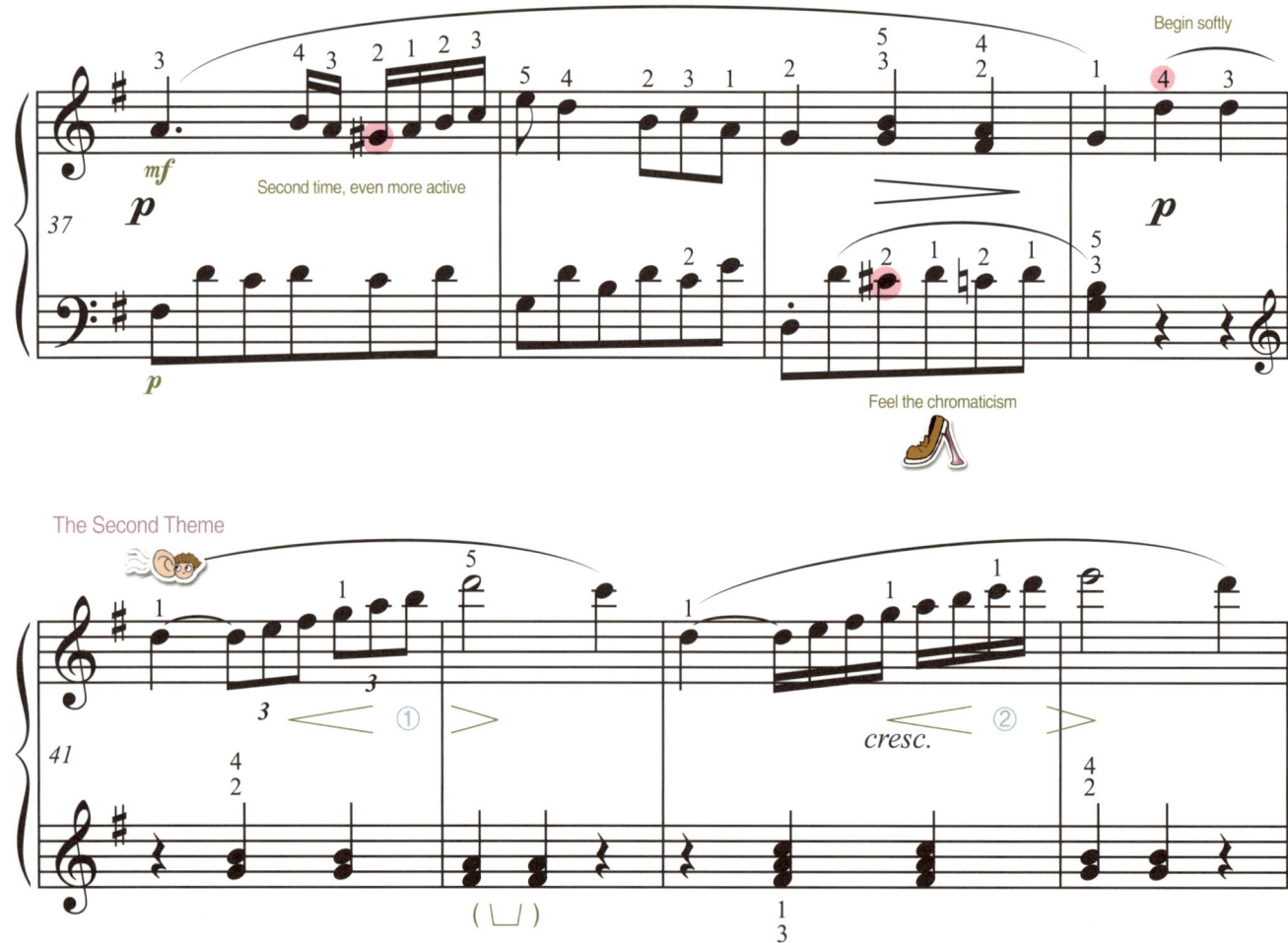

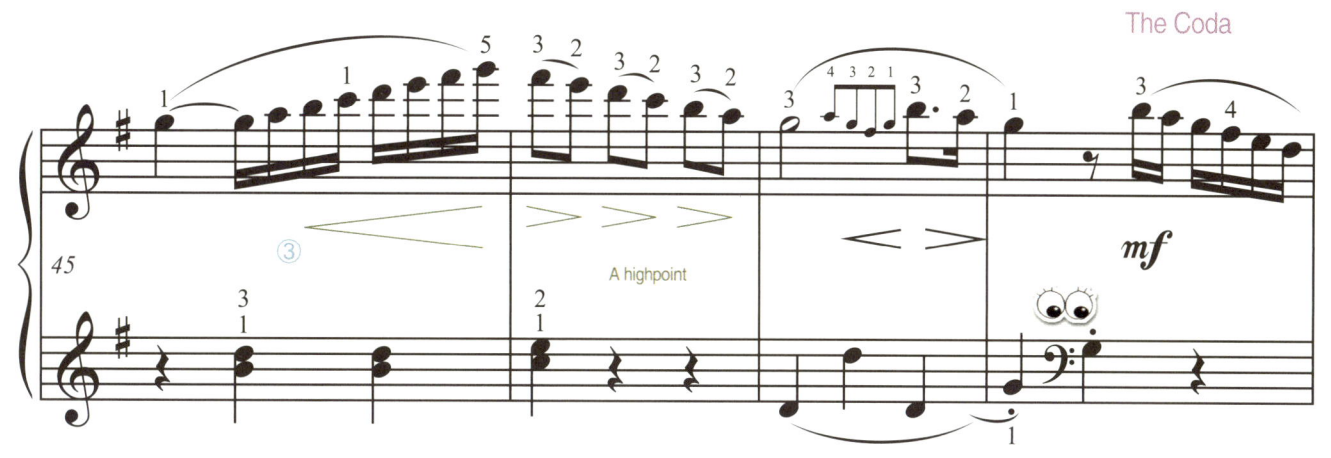

Kuhlau Sonatine

Op. 55 No. 2 in C Major, 2nd Movement

Ms. Silverplate's Smart Tips

🌼 **How do I make chromatic scales expressive?**

- With chromatic scales, you have to alternate between black and white keys almost at random. So it's important to have the correct hand posture and a flexible wrist.

- In most cases, chromatic scales need to feel slightly sticky and even romantic. Apply weight on your fingertips and have them close to the keyboard. Also, if you play the first note softly and then do a crescendo, the chromatic scales will be even fancier!

🌼 **The scale with the 6th interval is difficult to play fast!**

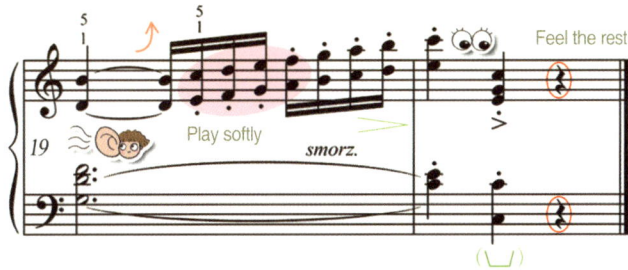

Here, you also need a firm palm and a flexible wrist. Play the 6ths as softly as you can.

- First, determine the distance between the two notes in the interval. Then maintain a firm hand shape.

- Let the first four chords after the tied 16th-note be very soft, so that your arm doesn't get tense.

> **Level up!** There is a similar passage in the 3rd movement of Beethoven's Sonata Op. 2 No. 3. Try it!

Kuhlau Op. 55 No. 2, 2nd movt.

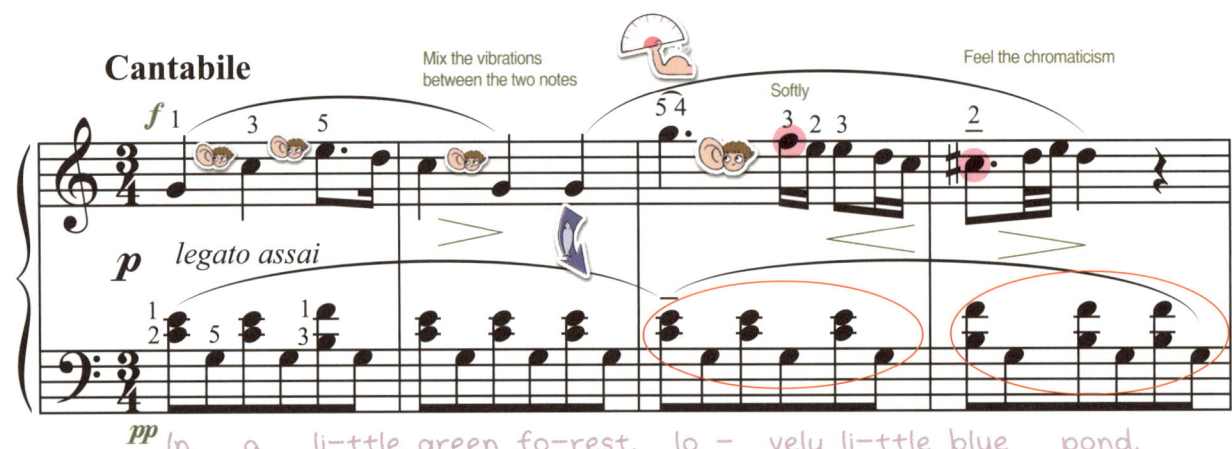

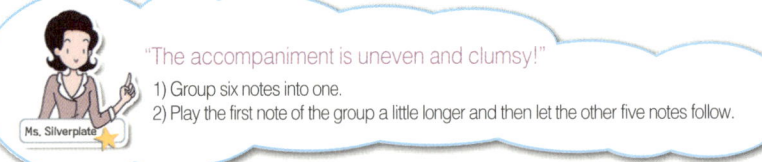

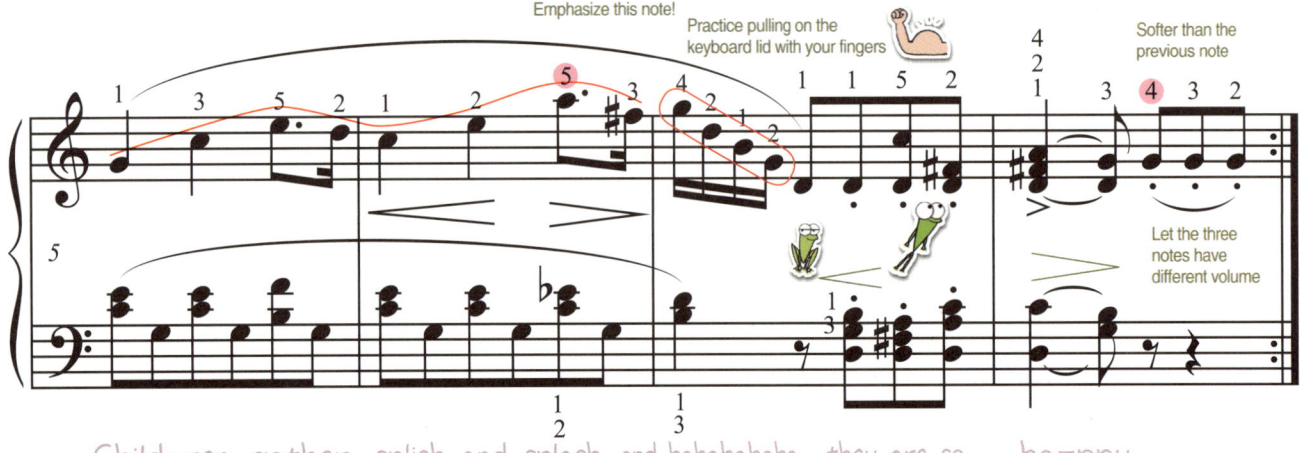

121

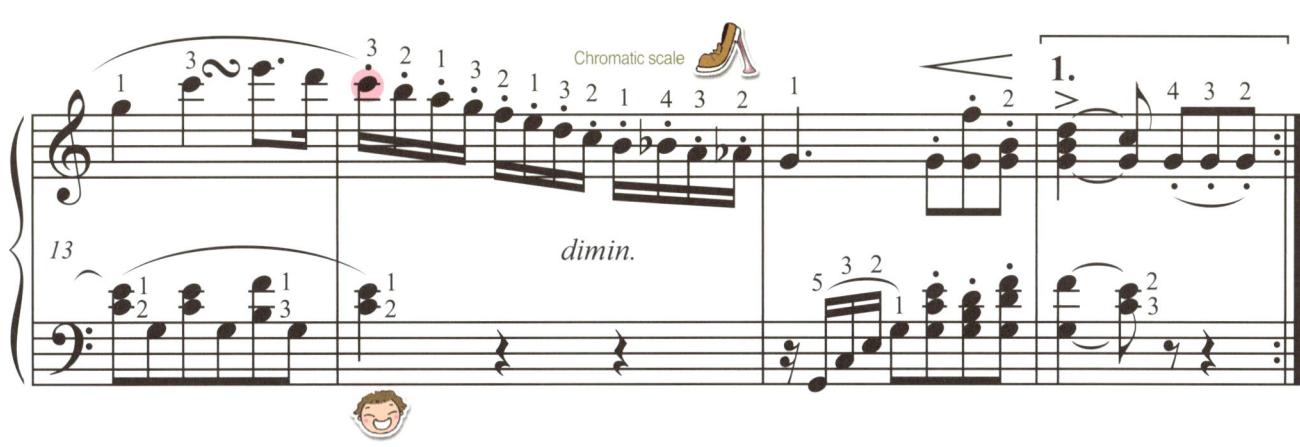

Sonatine Story

The secrets to solid, beautiful sound!
Stamina of a lion

It's already our last lesson. I applaud you for having followed diligently through with Sonatine Stories.
In this session, I'll teach you how to shape your hands so that you can create a healthy sound. Read along and try these tips!

1. Importance of knuckles

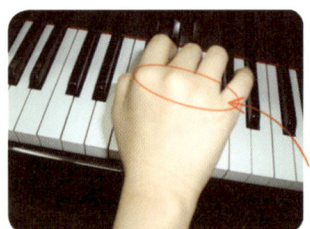

The knuckles

The knuckles on your hands must be visibly protruding in order for you to go to the next step...

2. Building a firm foundation

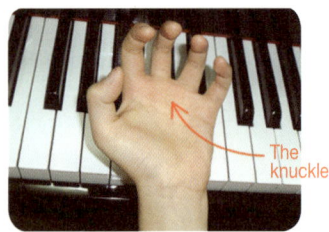

The knuckles

Your hand must be round and caved-in

Turn your hand so that you can see your palm.
The knuckle joints exist on the palm side of your hand as well.
Shape your hand so that your knuckle joints on the palm side go inward.

3. Feel that muscle!

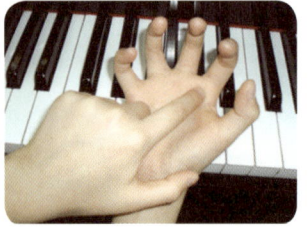

Firm muscles

If your hand has the right posture, bend each of your fingers (2, 3, 4 and 5) to make sure that the muscles on your knuckle joints have become firm.
You must remember this feeling.

4. Extracting sound

Release tension

The wrist joint

Immediately before playing, get into position

This is the moment we've all been waiting for. Is your hand ready with a strong posture and fingertips?
Then slightly pull your wrist backward and pull sound out of the key with your fingertips.
As you do this, your arm will go slightly forward.

Ms. Silverplate

if you try to maintain this strong posture all the time, your arms will hurt after a while and your sound will not come out.
Relax before playing, and then get into position right before playing.

Memo

About the Author

Dr. Joy Jeehai Song

Native of South Korea, Dr. Joy J. Song is regarded as an innovator in the field of piano pedagogy. She started the piano at age five and received her Bachelor's and Master's degree (and is currently waiting to receive a DMA) in Piano Performance. In addition to her performing career, she began taking interest in pedagogy and released acclaimed teaching books including *Nine Gifts by Piano Teachers*, *Secrets of Piano Scales* and *Kingdom of DaCapo: the Fairytale Piano Method*. After 25 years of teaching, she also earned a doctoral degree in Piano Pedagogy and soon began pursuing studies in a wide variety of fields, such as Early Childhood Development, Music Education and Christian Counseling.

Educational & Career Profile

- Bachelor's degree in Piano Performance with high honors: Yonsei University
- Master of Fine Arts in Piano Performance: UCLA
- Doctorate in Piano Pedagogy: AMC Graduate School
- Doctor of Musical Arts Program in Piano Performance (ABD): UCLA
- Additional postgraduate studies at California State University, Fullerton, University of Southern California, Horizon Institute & Patten University
- Head of Department & Professor: Sookmyung Women's University
- Adjunct Professor: Hansei University
- Lecturer: Seoul National University (Piano Teacher's program), Hyupsung University, Yonsei University, Chung-Ang University, EwhaWomen's University, Yewon School, Seoul Arts High School
- Director: Korea Institute of Piano Pedagogy
- Coach & Lecturer: MBTI Personality Types, Enneagram, DISC, Empowering Coach

Other books by Dr. Song

- Piano Pedagogy:
    - *Piano Method: Hibis*
    - *Nine Gifts by a Piano Teacher*
    - *Secrets of Piano Scales*
    - *Pearl's Scale*
    - *Kingdom of Da Capo*
    - *Cosmic Hanon*
    - *Scale for the Professional Pianist*
- Psychology:
    - *Happiness through Personality Types: Know your Spouse's Personality Type*
    - *Happiness through Personality Types: Know your Children's Personality Types*
    - *What Do You Really Want?: Core Needs of Each Personality Type*

 Translator: Yoon-Jee Kim, Conductor & Pianist (www.yoon-jee.com)

Welcome to the Icon village !
Name those Icons!

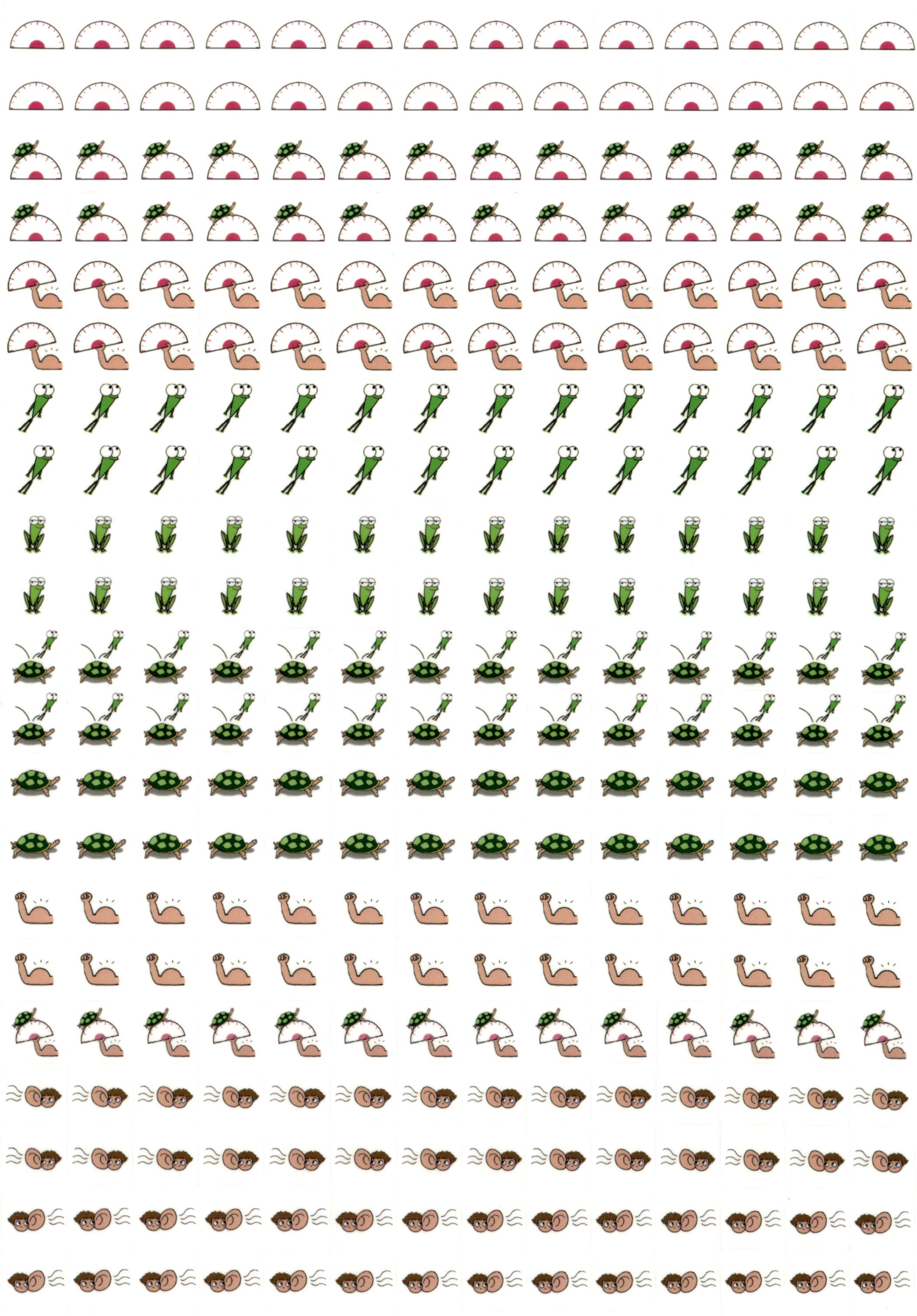

Welcome to the Icon village 2
Name those Icons!

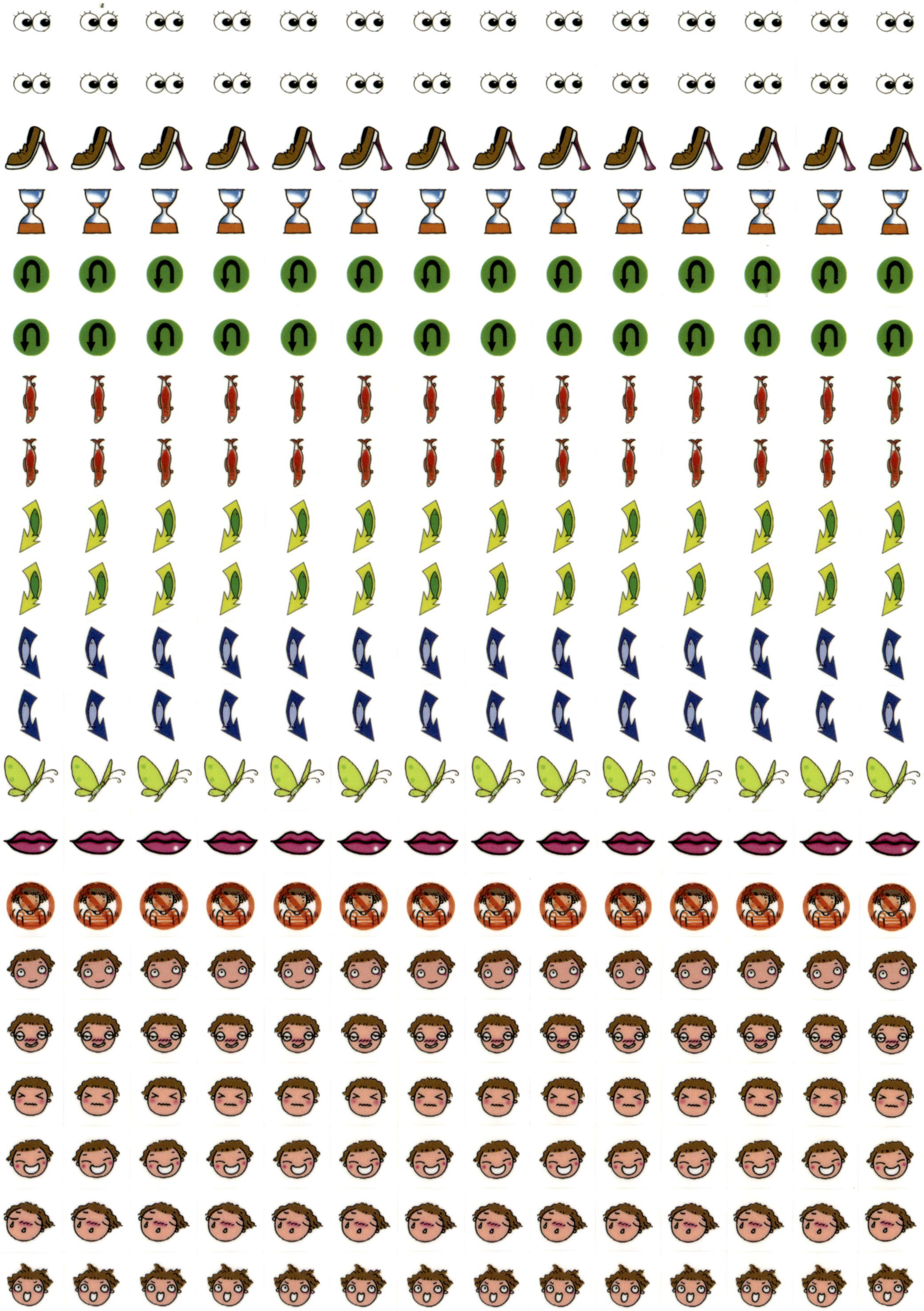